Good Idea! Now What?

How to Turn Your Idea, Invention, or Business Concept Into a Money-Making Success!

Howard Bronson

Good Idea!
Now What?

"ONE OF THE MOST SOUGHT-AFTER MARKETING EXPERTS IN THE COUNTRY. . . . A STEP-BY-STEP GUIDE TO MARKETING NEW IDEAS."—*Inland Business*

IF YOU'VE EVER HAD AN IDEA FOR A BUSINESS, PRODUCT, OR INVENTION, THIS BOOK IS FOR YOU!

Howard Bronson has helped thousands of individuals and corporations launch new business concepts and products. In this clearly written book he shows you how you can do it, too, by learning:

- What it takes to start a business or market an invention —and how you can do it without spending a fortune!

- The secrets of working with others, listening to feedback, and benefiting from professional expertise

- How to write your own professional press releases—to reach the right people with your idea

- How to attract nationwide attention with a powerful, FREE publicity campaign

- The ins and outs of pricing, selling, and distributing your product

- The simple rules of judging an idea—before you start marketing it.

Your creativity could be worth a fortune. Howard Bronson's GOOD IDEA! NOW WHAT? shows you how to start building your dream today!

Good Idea! Now What?

HOWARD BRONSON

WARNER BOOKS

A Warner Communications Company

Warner Books Edition
Copyright ©1986, 1987, 1988, 1989 by Howard Bronson

Permission should be addressed in writing to:
Bestsell Publications, 337 High Wood Way, New Seabury, Massachusetts 02649

This Warner Books edition is published by arrangement with Bestsell Publications.

Warner Books, Inc., 666 Fifth Avenue, New York, NY 10103

 A Warner Communications Company

Printed in the United States of America
First Warner Books Printing: January 1990
10 9 8 7 6 5 4 3 2 1

Cover design by Mike Stromberg

Library of Congress Cataloging-in-Publication Data

Bronson, Howard F., 1953-
    Good idea! now what? / Howard F. Bronson. — Warner Books ed.
      p. cm.
    Reprint. Originally published: Mashpee, Mass. : Bestsell
Publications, c1986.
    ISBN 0-446-39094-1 (pbk) (U.S.A. and Can.)
    1. Marketing—Management.   2. New products—Marketing.   3. Success
in business.   I. Title.
[HF5415.13.B73   1990]
658.8—dc20
                                         89-38251
                                            CIP

"If you have built castles in the air, your work need not be lost; that is where they should be.

Now put the foundations under them."

Henry David Thoreau

Preface

When I first had the idea to write *Good Idea! Now What?*, I presented rough drafts to top-notch professionals in many fields.

These ad execs, marketing consultants and other business pros all had the same passionate reaction. They hated it, and worse. They all felt the idea of starting or augmenting a business through free or almost free publicity was unrealistic.

Well, I listened to all these passionately opinioned folks, but luckily I trusted my own instincts just a little more, believing that millions of dreamers were getting a raw deal, that too many great ideas were dying unnecessarily, and that money was being wasted by people who just didn't realize that much of their marketing and development could be done for little or no money, people spending ten or twenty thousand dollars for a limited radio or TV tour or for various print publicity campaigns that never produced results. Now those same people are achieving much better results while investing only a few hundred dollars or less.

There are so many things that you can do to bring your idea to life. Don't let it die—you have no excuses now. This book is your marketing conditioner. Be patient and flexible and, most important,—enjoy!

Table of Contents

DEDICATION

In the down times of my life, my father used to grab me by the shoulders, look me square in the eye and say in an even and very assertive tone, "I don't care how many times you may fall flat on your face. As long as you keep getting up to try again, you will succeed."

On the evening of November 11, 1983, the life of this vigorous man was suddenly taken, sending a shock wave that will forever reverberate in the souls of his family and friends.

He gave me the strength to think and work toward success and to start this book.

Thanks, Gordon Bronson. I can still see your sparkle in the eyes of your grandchildren.

And to my courageous mother, Irma who has instilled in me the desire to pursue that success with compassion as well as passion.

Introduction

Every Tuesday at Twelve Noon, The U.S. Patent Office in Arlington, Virginia issues some 1,500 patents to individuals or businesses. These original creations or improvements on existing ones could be a better chocolate-chip cookie or a system to power artifical hearts with a patient's own stomach acid.

That's a lot of patents each year and that doesn't include the billions of inspirations that race in and out of our heads daily. And what about the thousands of business or community ventures begun each day. How many actually amount to something?

Think of the times you've had a great idea that died simply because you didn't know how easily you could turn that thought into profit. Most of us, even those who get to the patent stage, do not know how to bring our ideas successfully to market. One or two naive attempts and we sour on the whole process.

The idea fizzles out and our productivity and hopes are diminished. Worst of all, the world never gets the benefit of what could have made life more productive, safer, more profitable or more enjoyable.

But there are many ways to make your ideas come to life and they are neither expensive nor complicated. In fact, many of my high credibility production and advertising systems are virtually free. Well, actually there are a few minor expenses for hefty high-tech equipment such as pencils, stamps, clay, telephone calls, paper, things like that.

These are systems that work and have indeed worked for countless clients from Cape Cod to China. I have small Mom and Pop clients who have saved hundreds of dollars. I also have some big clients who have saved hundreds of thousands of dollars by adopting my systems.

Hundreds of people come to me each year with ideas, either in the dream stage or out of the patent-office. As I'm sure yours are, most of these ideas are wonderful and clever and I always wished I had the resources to develop all of them.

Because I didn't have the time to help each of you personally, I decided to write this book and develop a personal follow-up program to assist you in promoting yourself and your ideas.

I will prove to you that you can do it cheaply but with a powerful degree of credibility and effectiveness.

If you're an individual adventurist, this book is perfect for you because it will give you the development and exposure power without the big financial risk.

If you run a company or any type of organization, be it tiny, medium or ultra-large, I have a challenge for you: The next time you have a new product or service you may want to develop and introduce to the public, have your agency employ my techniques as a test. The money you save could forever change the way you use the services of an ad or publicity agency.

Some of you will use this book to develop that artificial heart battery or that better chocolate-chip cookie (please hurry!). I spent years researching and refining these techniques and now I want to share them with you.

You will need spirit, patience and a good sense of humor. You will have to learn how to listen and then make your own final decisions.

I will take you step by step along a path that can make your dreams happen. Occasionally, you'll be subjected to a brief story from my career to help you understand a concept or avoid a costly mistake. If you're willing to live many of my stories vicariously, you can profit from my blunders without having to pay for them.

If this is your first venture, great. You've come to the right place. I'll show you how to exploit your imagination without exploiting your wallet. If you've been in any aspect of this business for a while, I hope my systems will compliment and enhance your existing skills.

Regarding those of you who have already made it and have purchased this book to refine or streamline techniques, that knowledge should come as encouraging news to those of you who are just starting out. No matter who you are, you're getting marketing information that's easy to follow yet so effective, the pros use it.

You hear about successful people who perpetually praise the free-enterprise system. It's worked for them and it can work just as beautifully for you especially if you employ my techniques.

There is no talent barrier here. You could be a scientist, a hobbyist or housewife. In fact, I get a lot of letters from housewives who often feel that they don't have what it takes to make their ideas successful.

That claim especially makes no sense to me. Any woman who can manage a home and/or family has already proven that she is extremely capable.

All anyone needs to begin is either a realistic dream or the willingness to explore the possibility of creating one. The realization of every person's dream is an American birthright but the proper steps must be taken to profit from that dream.

So do you have to be a ruthless or legal thief to get rich on your ideas? Of course not, though there are many vultures on this Earth. I'm proud to count not one of these types as my friends.

Luck? Hard work? Dedication? Real Estate? Inheritance? What's the formula? Well, did you ever stop to think that after you've heard all those platitudes for success, you still haven't learned a thing about personal success?

Statistics indicate that more than half of you have purchased some type of "How To Succeed" book at some point in your life. Statistics also show that most of those books didn't deliver what they promised. So I have really got my work cut out for me.

I've read many of the management, marketing and real estate "How To's." In my humble opinion, I think you bought the right one because I don't just throw you a few tips and expect you to create miracles. I, in fact, help you evolve your venture with solid systems for your success while also maintaining a sensitivity to your fears of success.

This is one "How To" book that reaches a helping hand to you right out of its pages and right when you need it most. And just as you will adopt these techniques for many ventures throughout your life, my staff of seasoned consultants are always available to help you resolve any special hurdles.

My job is to team up with your imagination and make your idea sell. I am unconventional. I reserve the right to break some of my own rules in the name of venture success. I hope you will break some of my rules when you find it necessary.

I'll be with you step by step, chapter by chapter. If you stumble, get up and try again. If you can learn what made you fall you can continue to grow with your dreams.

Approach your project with courage and confidence no matter what the odds and no matter what anyone tells you. This book can be useful at any level. I don't care how stupid or smart you are, unless you think you're too smart to take good advice. Our goal is to take your good idea and successfully make it grow and get it to the marketplace.

All I ask is that you stick with the book, that you not be discouraged, that you not let fears of failure close you down to the success you deserve and the success you will have.

Here's a nice quote from Coolidge to start us off on the right foot:

Press On

"Nothing in the world can take the place of persistence.
TALENT will not: Nothing is more common than unsuccessful men with talent.
GENIUS will not: Unrewarded genius is almost a proverb.
EDUCATION alone will not: The world is full of educated derelicts.
PERSISTENCE and DETERMINATION alone are omnipotent."

Chapter 1

HOW TO FIND YOUR IDEA
Are You Where You Wanna Be?

The Caribbean night sky was bleeding stars. I had just finished an exhausting stint writing and producing radio ads for The American Express "Do You Know Me" account so the peace of this island was thrilling.

It was easy to hire a fisherman to take me and my date on a night cruise aboard his tiny boat. The stars cast a silver glow over the water but it wasn't enough for us to see that piece of shark net out of place. The little boat jerked to a stop as its motor snagged on the net.

The sharks gathering around the boat seemed even more thrilled than I was since we must have looked very appetizing. We couldn't move, couldn't get the engine free and couldn't row because we forgot the oars.

It was Hell in paradise and I pushed us into it. Just as my date was pledging to kill me if the sharks didn't eat us first, another small boat appeared in the night. "Are you where you wanna be?" the islander asked.

Oh sure we were. My date just loved being stuck with hungry sharks.

Are you where you want to be? That's our first task and it is the most important.

"I have a great idea!" lightbulb flashing over your head, eyes as big as tomatoes. Everyone's had some kind of inspiration in their lives but the trick is to keep that lightbulb burning bright.

If you already have your heart set on an idea, let's take a

closer look at it to make sure you'll want to stay with it. If you don't have an idea in mind yet, that's fine. We'll take a closer look at how we all develop ideas and open ourselves up to the process.

For Square 1, you must promise never to limit your imagination. Maybe you've had a few brainstorms in your life. Maybe not and at this point you really don't know if you have anything you can really develop and market.

I can tell you that everyone has some gift that they could market successfully. Is it that special cake or little tool you make for neighbors? Maybe it's your talent for solving conflicts or an idea to make your community a better place to live. It's there. You just have to recognize what you've always had and then couple it with the processes outlined in the next two chapters.

Creativity is the exploration of possibilities. You have to learn to play a game of "what-ifs" and play it to the max. If you're not willing to take the simple mental risk of astounding and shocking yourself, you run the risk of never really surprising or delighting yourself.

There are many books that will attempt to offer you specific categories and systems to help you define your talents. I find this practice horribly limiting. One of my greatest reasons for my successes is that I never let anyone corral me into just one specific area.

I have earned a certain degree of freedom and control over my life and you can have the same privilege as you learn to celebrate your personal potential and initiative. This is a free country. Don't be anyone's slave.

If your idea doesn't begin to gel after the first chapter, put this book down and don't continue until you have one that you really want to work with. That may take a few days or months. The delay makes no difference unless you're under a killer deadline.

In 1983 and 84, I was involved in the marketing of all the officially licensed Olympic products. My 20 Olympic product accounts each had firm time frames for selling. The day after the Olympics, most of these products (with the exception of some collectibles) were obsolete.

What an accelerated marketing education that was! I had to find markets in a very compressed time frame. I should have gotten a gold medal for all the headaches I had to put up with. I settled for the money instead.

I could tackle the Olympics because I had worked up to it. But I didn't start there. I started with individual products within reasonable time constraints, just as you will be doing.

Begin carrying a little notebook around with you and make notes about any ideas you may want to pursue. What are the dreams and wishes that make sense to your lifestyle? And you know those thoughts that breeze in and out of your head? Write them down.

Every spark counts when you are in the selection process. The human creative process seems to throw fragments your way as if from nowhere and you find yourself almost automatically saying, "Nah, that's crazy."

From now on when any of these notions whiz by, stop them in their tracks and write them down. Never say "Nah."

Every week or so, dump these notes on a table and try to see if some of these fragments are beginning to suggest an overall picture of what your venture may be.

Don't make copious notes and there should be very little anxiety involved. Just gently plant a few seeds here and there and keep checking for patterns. Look and listen in your own style. You're aiming to grow with something that's going to be an important part of "where you want to be."

Don't limit yourself just because you think a problem or goal seems a bit large in scope. Writing this book seemed scary to me until I began attacking it page by page until I one day found myself with a book.

That process will happen with your idea. As your

thoughts develop, you begin to get a strong sense of what you'll work with. Often people come up with ventures that outwardly seem to have no relevancy to their lives. Real wishes are often break away hidden loves that need to be properly guided.

Too busy, lazy, sick, whatever. That makes no difference because the right idea will spark ample motivation.

Hang up your hang-ups and take advantage of that incredible American gift of free thought and exploration. Many people have never allowed themselves to have a free thought in their lives but it's so easy to learn how. Let your mind wander. You can always come back.

Go out and live your life as you normally do. Start off by simply thinking about possibilities. In no time, you'll find that you have more ideas than you ever gave yourself credit for. That discovery generally comes as a refreshing and motivating surprise.

Keep at it until you have really found something that you will nurture and market, something that you can grow with. Remember, if it is "Where you want to be," you'll find the wherewithal to stay with it.

To continue shaping your idea, let's make a Three-Stage Wish. Real wishes usually come true but you have to know how to make a real wish.

STAGE 1. If I asked most of you to make any wish, most of you would wish for lots of money. Most people are indeed stuck in the first stage.

I have nothing against lotteries, in fact, maybe our income taxes should be replaced with mandatory lotteries. But "Lottery People" who hope that some freak remote chance will drape them in clover, rarely succeed. One must get past the first stage because hope alone won't produce our success.

STAGE 2 of our wish is that thing we want to improve, that problem that we want to attack. What specific area of your world would you like to improve?

Maybe you want to communicate better with your family or find a way to realize increased employee productivity. Maybe you want to develop a new or improved product or service. What about a way to do your small part to make the world safer for children? Let's work with the "safer children" notion as STAGE 2 of our wish. Following is an actual example of how one of my clients brought this to the third stage.

A rather brilliant man presented his concept to me by first telling a story about a girl he knew who dove into a swimming pool and was instantly and horribly electrocuted due to a frayed wire in an underwater pool switch. He vowed that he would muster his gifts to make sure such a nighmare would never happen again.

He channeled his passion into the development of an underwater safety switch that eliminated electrical contact near the pool area. The product he created and I marketed represents the vital STAGE 3 of our wish and that's what you want to head to. Be it a product or service, STAGE 3 represents your plan of attack.

It makes no difference how simple or complicated your idea is. Everyone has the ability to act upon some idea that's personally important and/or just plain fun. Everyone I have ever met has some idea they want to develop and market. There has never been a more favorable climate as there is today for personal success. Coupled with my low-cost development and marketing systems, your personal possibilities are greater than ever.

This is not mere psychological cheerleading. Look at all the magazines and news items that now feature new products or services. There is clearly an increasingly receptive market for ideas from the individual dreamer and I will show you the path of least resistance to get your share.

If you really want your idea to succeed, you must have a love affair with your idea and falling in love takes some time. So take the time. No success in sixty seconds here.

When you finish with this book, I want you to have more than just gimmickry. I want you to have something of value that celebrates your personal initiative. That's where I want you to be. That's my STAGE 3.

Do you have your idea locked down? The right idea? If you think so, let's see if it will hold up through the next chapter. But so far, you're doing great. If you're following my system, aside from the cost of this book, your only expenses so far have been for pencils and notepads and you probably already had those.

Chapter 2

HOW TO TEST YOUR IDEA
Getting Expensive Results Without The Expense

Alfred Hitchcock. The name immediately evokes an entire concept. His genius of suspense, his almost extrasensory ability to thrill and delight you.

In August of 1976, I had the good fortune of meeting him. It was late at night of course. We were both vacationing at the Mauna Kea resort in Hawaii. I walked into the seaside bar for a late night drink and there he was, alone, solemn, yet somehow approachable.

It was a Hawaiian-style, open air bar with rustling tropical plants wiggling their leaves, like a thousand dancing fingers.

A mysterious darkness seemed to prevail, with most of the illumination coming from the little enclosed table candles. One of these candles cast an eerie glow under Mr. Hitchcock's face.

I had every reason to turn and run. The sense of danger, the awesomeness of a celebrity. What could a young fan like me say to such a complete master who actually seemed to control the environment! I asked him if he wanted some company and he said, "Yes!" (Does it pay to take a chance or what!)

I can still recite that twenty-minute conversation, word-for-word and describe every nuance. I was a young writer and had yet to discover the focus of my talent.

During one segment of that conversation, I asked him outright what advice he could give a young upstart writer who wanted to be commercially successful.

"My dear boy," he slowly turned toward me as he spoke, that underlighting now giving him a more-than-human appearance. In that great warm and authoritative soft British bellow, he continued, "You've got to know what your audience is theeenking."

Know what your audience is thinking. That was my first lesson in the development of a major selling point of my career. What do they want out there and how can I give it to them?

Learning to develop good ideas has been a specialty of mine. Why do some grow and others die? Interestingly enough, Hitchcock helped take the mystery out of it for me. Now I know how to do my homework.

So here you are. You think you're all ready to forge ahead and see if your idea will hold water.

Do you really have a good idea? I'm going to be a little harsh on you for a bit to help reduce your chances of expending your energies in the wrong direction and should the idea hold water, help you every way I can in the right direction.

If I send you back to the first chapter, it's only to increase your chances of success. If you don't agree with me, that's your right. Answer the following questions honestly:

Is your idea something you just thought of the other day? You may have said to yourself, "Yeah, that's as good an idea as any." Does this describe you at all? That's fine. Go back to CHAPTER 1 and start over.

Are you ready to risk a chunk of your hard-earned money in your idea? You are? Okay, you're demoted. You may be too anxious to see your idea clearly. Go back and make sure you've thought it through. Take the time to give your inspirations a healthy birth.

Are you afraid of failure? Are you worried that your idea may not work out and that you'll be wasting your time? Let me tell you. I sure am. I want everything I do to lead to success. Note that I have used the word "lead." Failures are nothing more than temporary detours on your path to success. They are just one crucial component of the success formula. Wear your faults like a badge. If you understand what went wrong and how to make it right, you'll continually be able to promote your cause.

All businesses are in business to solve a particular problem. They attempt to turn that problem into an opportunity and hence, profit. See how important your failures can be?

So, you're confident enough about your idea to have continued on. What would a major advertising agency or marketing company do at this point? If they liked the idea, they might spend thousands of dollars, at the very least, to test the concept, then design, develop, promote and get it out to market.

Many concepts die very expensive deaths, not always because they are bad products. The successful development of a product or service depends on the creative and technical abilities or limitations of that particular developer.

Bad planning, bad feedback, and most importantly, bad listening wastes money. Bad listening destroys spaceships and melts nuclear reactors. We must do our share to avoid that whether we are developing a product for a company or ourselves.

First of all, aside from yourself, determine who your idea will benefit. If you think it's only the user, think again. What about the distributors, manufacturers, all of the people involved in the production of the item before it reaches its final destination?

Before we get into my preliminary testing phase, there are many readers who are afraid that someone out there may just steal their idea. Most of the time, you'll find that people are trustworthy but, to put your mind at ease, you could do the following: Write down a brief description of your concept, including any supporting documentation. Make two copies and mail one to your lawyer and one to yourself.

They are to be kept sealed until needed.

If your idea is sufficiently unique, have your attorney begin the patent process. Additionally, if you are exploring your idea with a potential maker, you can ask him to sign a statement that he will not replicate the idea you are about to discuss.

Whatever you do, don't be too paranoid. After all, you're going to become so knowledgeable about your concept, you'll be the authority.

When I come up with a new marketing scheme or product, I'm generally flattered and amused by my imitators; flattered because they copied my idea and amused because they can rarely do it as well or as cost-effectively as I can.

In short, people are desperate for good ideas because they haven't learned to develop their own creative process by following my guidelines. They are afraid of the idea of the creative process. These types of people don't generally have what it takes to make an idea happen because they are not really a part of its birth. Thieves always get caught, either by others or themselves.

But all philosophy aside, remember in business ventures, there is only one definition of a gift. A gift is any work, money, anything you contribute without a written agreement in advance. Always find a way to move ahead but don't ever downplay the need to protect yourself.

A long time ago, I invoked the postmark protection for a great idea of mine. It was a toothbrush with a toothpaste cartridge built right in. You just press a button and your toothbrush is loaded and ready to brush. I even made a prototype to show to a manufacturer. Then a day before my presentation, I was in a local drug store and noticed that a similar product was already on the market. I later found out it had been on the market long before I ever thought of it.

So, if you're putting together a product, make sure that exact product is not already on the market. As long as you make an improvement or some significant modification, then you should be able to get your patent, if necessary and move forward.

Millions of you have service or product ideas that may not require a patent. For the particular state you're living in, an attorney would best advise you in all areas of product protection.

It will take a lot more homework before your idea is actually ready for the development stages. We don't know exactly what we've got yet. Over and over again, I will remind you to keep thinking results, don't get stuck.

Time to pick some brains. There are scores of people out there who will be only too glad to give you free time and advice. FREE ADVICE. Some of it will be questionable but some of it will prove highly valuable. As you become more intimate with your product, and if you use this book as a guide, you'll soon learn to decipher the useable from the stuff you throw away.

I said free advice. Why will so many experts generally be glad to give you some free time? If your product takes off, some of these people know they may become involved in the production process. A little investment of their time could really pay off.

Tell these valued advisors what you are thinking of and make notes. You're not always going to like what you hear but a little criticism can save you a fortune. Remember that underwater safety switch I described in the last chapter? Here's a good lesson: AFTER we gave the distributors thousands of these single switches, we met with them to find out how it was doing. Unanimously, they told us there was no market for a single switch, only a DOUBLE, high capacity system. Had we picked their brains before we hit the drawing board, the client would have saved a lot of time and money.

Pick brains FIRST. Talk to authorities. Don't assume you know it all just because you were successful in another career. A number of my clients are in their sixties and seventies and are wealthy. Almost invariably, the first thing I work to convey to them is, just because they turned sixty, that doesn't automatically make them an authority on everything.

However, in no way will I ever deny that one of your greatest potential assets for procedural guidance could be the great and untapped wealth of retired persons and senior citizens. Seek them out via your local senior citizens organizations. Generally, you'll make some great friends and your product will enjoy a much better end result to success.

Very often, I tap into my consortium of seniors when I am undertaking a new venture. When I used to live in Los Angeles, I had a next-door neighbor named Howard Miller. I can tell you that he didn't reach his nineties by being anybody's fool. What a privileged life I had to have had so much wisdom right next door.

Wisdom is knowledge of what is true or correct coupled with good judgement. It's the ultimate reward for all your triumphs and your screw-ups. In fact, I learned so much more from the mistakes of others, than from even my own cache of faux pas. Keep the following in mind: As long as your idea has some merit to someone, there's always a way to put it together. Listen, think and accept no one as final authority except yourself.

I actually know someone who spent almost One Hundred Fifty Thousand Dollars to make a mold for the mass production of his product in plastic. Any injection-molder will tell you that he could make a similar mold for only a few hundred dollars.

I've discussed basic products so my points would be clearly understood. But many readers have very complex ideas or services. Essentially, the same query-approaches apply. In fact, if your idea is service-oriented, you can often see the possibilities blossoming at a very rapid rate.

Let's suppose you want to create an information source

for local Senior Citizens. You might begin by discussing it with a local senior center, or even city hall. Such was the case in New Bedford, Massachusetts. A housewife, whose children had grown and left the nest wound up successfully getting start-up funds and now runs a newspaper exclusively for Seniors.

She had done some writing in the past and she wanted to make a useful contribution to her community. Her paper is now a model for similar efforts around the country. All she began with was an intelligent idea that complimented her potential, and a little homework. What a perfect inspiration and example of finding one's star.

Some people may call some of my research tactics a form of networking. It's actually a form of reverse consulting. Networking implies talking business at parties. I don't like that. For now, when you're at a party, have fun. Go easy on your friends. You want customer reaction but spread your inquiries around or you'll be the death of any party.

Take Hitchcock's advice. Talk to potential customers. What do they want from a better widget? And what about the existing product that may be similar to yours. What's wrong with it and why is yours an improvement over it? What are the problems that you can eliminate? Ask, Explore, LISTEN and Digest. Keep thinking Concept, Research, Refine the Concept, Focus the Research.

As you progress in this area, something exciting begins to happen. Your ideas begin to come into focus. As the dust settles you have begun to get a much better idea of where you're going and how to get there. Best of all, you haven't spent thousands of dollars to test your market or shape your gem. For this chapter, you have spent some money on gas, phone calls and some more pads and pencils. That's a reasonable investment to explore your dream.

How's your concept building? Are you ready to make it come to life? Let's find out.

Chapter 3

DEVELOPMENT & ASSESSMENT
Creating A Model

Science fiction films have become so creative and convincing, we essentially accept their portrayals of the future as gospel. Deep space adventures are presented with a clever intermesh of intelligence, compassion and photon torpedos.

No space vehicle or home will be complete without a transporter which will demolecularize any human or object and make it come to life at any other given point in the universe.

Items like transporters seem light years away with no bearing on today's world.

Star Trek has landed and I have seen it alive at the GE Plastics Technology Division in Pittsfield, Massachusetts.

Things of all types, born of ideas are transformed from the center of the mind onto a computer screen, where it may be plainly seen from all perspectives. It does not stop there.

Right there, within the heart of the computer, the image can be engineered, even to the point of stress analysis and performance testing.

Turn on the transporter. Here comes the real magic. Before thousands of dollars have been spent drafting, testing, etc., the computer actually transforms the design into a physical product mold, from which the product can be made.

Computer aided design and engineering is carried out at many levels in many companies throughout the world. These are the ultimate dream-into-reality machines riding on the leading edge of the future. But they cannot tell us if the people will actually accept a product no matter how perfect it may be.

I shall assume that most readers do not yet have access to such million-dollar technology but we shall still achieve viable test results well within or below your budget.

You're about to discover the vast difference between image and substance. The development process is also the second phase of the evaluation process. Here is where we beam our ideas into something real.

You've kicked your idea around with everyone. Some of your friends will think you're really into something interesting. Some think you're all talk. Attitudes will really change as your image transforms into substance.

How do you build a model if you've never built one before? Do you begin at the beginning? Not necessarily. But you must begin.

In college I took a few art courses. Though I contend it was to escape from the pressures of my other studies, my poor art teachers will insist that I did it to prove that I was the world's worst artist.

I couldn't paint. I couldn't sculpt. I just never knew how to get a piece going. Finally, an artist got a hold of me. She gave me a brush, paints and a blank canvas and said, "Just throw something, anything on the canvas and don't think about it."

I did this for several sessions. I never became a very good artist. It's just not a gift of mine. I did continue to improve a little. The vital point is to let your models evolve no matter how sketchy or sloppy the beginning is. Remember the very adult message from Peter Pan: "If you don't dream, how will your dreams come true?"

Don't get so confused or rigid that you're afraid to begin. Now that your ideas are starting to come into focus, throw it on the canvas or paper or whatever. You probably won't love what you see at first. Doing is more important than asking why at this stage.

Even if the physical birth of your idea is a little ugly, don't worry about it. At least it's a birth. The first two chapters have already helped you build a wealth of knowledge. Don't be too disappointed at this stage. This is a time to be flexible.

Too many times in my career have I seen great ideas get trashed just as soon as its creator decides an obstacle is too great to overcome. This will happen a lot, especially with the development of a first project.

I have a buddy in Vermont named Skip Morrow. He was always subjecting us to nutty ideas and wacky illustrations. We all knew he was going someplace but we didn't know when he would actually be admitted.

Finally, he assembled some of his illustrations to create a comic calendar about cats. I thought the sketches were kind of cute until...

A few years passed when, in a bookstore one day, there it was: "The Official 'I Hate Cats' Book," written and illustrated by none other than Skip Morrow. Skip went on to enjoy many bestsellers and now creates a successful line of greeting cards, as well as a thousand other ideas.

He knew his talent, developed it and got it on paper. This creative genius took his rebellious, unconventional thoughts and stayed with them. Now instead of living in an institution, he has become one. Excited, alive and ever driven by his creativity. May we all reach that level one day.

If you don't try to make your idea happen, it will most likely never become real.

Your aim here is to create something that will help start the wheels of production turning. Don't cut corners. You could imagine that you could go to a particular manufacturer and tell him about and maybe sell him your concept. Most major manufacturers get this kind of proposal every day.

My experience has taught me that this is not the best way to make your product fly. As I mentioned earlier, consult with these heavies but assemble the overall technology yourself. The working or nearly-working model is of much greater financial benefit to you than just an idea.

You worked hard to get that idea! Are you just going to give it away — for a few dollars when you can make it yourself?

I get letters daily almost always containing these phrases; "I'm no mechanic. I'm no artist, I'm no sculptor. I'm afraid to approach person 'X'. I'm no writer."

In order to save a host of stamps, let me now respond collectively. I'm not interested in what you can't do, I'm only interested in working with what you've got. Just talk to these people as people and discover what you have in common.

If your idea is a physical product, make it — out of clay, or popsicle sticks, or wires, or whatever. Have fun. Relive your childhood. Creativity is fun because you're giving birth to something new that has never been done quite like you're doing it.

Once you feel you have a rough idea of what you wish your blob of clay would have looked like, take your blob to your local starving artist or sculptor or drafting student. Tell them what you were trying to do, get a solid price (anywhere from free to One Hundred Dollars, or find someone else) and a firm deadline (one-to-four weeks depending on the sophistication of your blob).

Warn your model-refiner that you may call once or twice with a few slight modifications. It's important to be clear about your thoughts and it's equally important for the artist to be sufficiently flexible in order make your idea happen. Establish a clear rapport from the beginning.

If your project requires a drawing, do what you can first, and then follow the above procedures.

Written descriptions can be a bit more traumatic for many but they shouldn't be. As you write, pretend you're writing a letter to your best friend or anyone else who you feel can understand what your thoughts mean. If you still have a problem, get a little tape recorder or dictaphone and talk away.

If your written proposal doesn't convey what it should to your particular target, bring it to your local high school English teacher. He'll refine and clarify your draft for free or for a modest fee (same formula as with models described earlier).

A few weeks later, you'll see the first signs of genuine encouragement for your project. That star we've been looking for and struggling with from page one suddenly is showing some promise of life.

When you get the preliminary phase in your hands, hold it, stare at it, sleep with it, make notes about it.

You can see how you're increasing the value of your idea for yourself. Aren't you glad you didn't run to the first major manufacturer you could find?

We're still in two phases simultaneously. Development and evaluation. As things develop, you evaluate, assess and make the appropriate modifications that permit you to move forward. Let's really get a jump on those manufacturers. Let's make a working model.

I don't care how well it works as long as it works. It merely has to make a point that it can do what you promise.

Look what you've done. You don't need an expert to tell you that it's not perfect. But is it something real that validates your dreams.

At this point, many of you are so excited that you're ready to go running to the nearest manufacturer or distributor. Instant wealth, fame or whatever. You've made it this far now all you want to do is get it out on the market.

Most of you however, are not ready yet to go to market. So if you begin to work with a manufacturer at this level of unreadiness, what happens to your credibility and value?

And if your idea is more in the service realm, all down on paper and ready to wow your prospects. Stop! Before you go rushing out there, you need your heaviest degree of informal "grand-round" advice.

Schedule a meeting with a group of potential producers of your idea. Before you meet with them, be sure your idea is adequately protected. Personally, I simply keep a written track record of all my concepts.

At this meeting, expect to be insulted. After all, your concept is a part of you, but you're looking for hard core critiques now before any big expense is involved. Write down a list of hard questions. Let them rip your idea to shreds. They may finally kick you out. They may make you an offer.

Whatever you hear, you'll make no decision at that point. You may now want to forget your entire idea or you may want to jump at the first offer you've heard. Instead, you will go home or go back to work and not think about your venture for a few days.

Then slowly digest all these new ideas. Your goal is to find a way to make your idea more viable. Some of you will destroy your original models and proposals. Some of you will make slight modifications. In either case, you will be finding ways to enhance the value of your product.

Keep it fun. Keep your sense of humor. Revel in the fact that throughout my career, I have already made the big mistakes for you. You have reached this crucial development stage without spending any significant money. Discouragement can and will be corrected but a squandered life-savings over a half-tested idea? We can avoid that.

I've seen it happen to people of all levels of intelligence. I wish they had had the sense to invest a few dollars in this book. Think of the money they could have saved and that's not the only loss. Their wonderful idea becomes only a bitter memory.

So no matter what stage you're at, and many of you will have suffered severe setbacks at this stage of the game, that doesn't matter. What does matter is the heightened awareness and education you now have about your idea. Your small failure is paving the way to a more genuine success.

Young or old, you don't have time to mourn your mistakes. Just learn from them and move forward. Remember, regret is the greatest waste of human resources!

A few years ago, one of my first cousins was dying of an inoperable brain tumor. He was a physician who was always trying to make a better widget. One of his final projects was the development of a more efficient tissue analysis unit.

Even in his final weeks of life, he was busily trying to get this project going. His wife is now putting the finishing touches on his invention.

So what's your excuse? Don't give up on an idea with potential. You may have to rechannel your energies a bit. You may even want to walk away from it all for a week or two. Take a mental vacation from it until you can approach it with a fresh attitude.

As a writer, I love my computer/word processor because it allows me to correct the same page as many times as I need to without any extra effort or time. I can give the impression of being able to take criticism well for any of my writing because my computer/word processor permits me to perfect my product without the traditional labor and frustration. Hence, I've learned the art of refining in a backwards manner.

The point is not to get a computer but of course, to patiently rework your model until the experts love it. That way you get the expert's stamp of approval but you still own the idea!

By sticking with my development advice, you've created some exciting options for yourself. You didn't sell out so as a reward you can now offer producers the option of "buying in."

Now you've got something and Chapter 4 will help you begin to make the best of it in some very exciting and profitable ways.

Chapter 4

PREPARATIONS FOR TESTING THE MARKET
Making It Go Without Letting It Go And The People Test

A few years ago, I witnessed the installation of the latest high-tech desalinization machinery at a popular Caribbean resort. Years of lab research had yielded the ultimate device for turning sea water into the purest drinking water imaginable, "Purer and tastier than spring water," as its developers told me.

They had a party to officially ordain this great machinery with gallons of converted water for all to test. Everyone seemed to have good things to say about this brilliantly engineered marvel.

When they asked me for my opinion, I said the first thing that came to my mind. "It still tastes a little salty." Everyone laughed except for its inventors who later discovered that their device did indeed have a problem.

A few weeks and several thousand dollars later, it was corrected after much embarrassment and the most essential test of all...the people test. No matter how perfect the lab results, the word of that end-user is your best teacher. Our aims are to avoid salty public embarrassments while we continue progressing.

You have made strides in developing your idea and now have to face the challenge of testing it while building your own personal value to any future prospect.

Can you imagine giving up rights and ownership of your idea only to discover that someone else ended up making a fortune on it. Just a few pennies for you. You didn't think you were capable of making it happen so you sold out. After you read this book, you should have an entirely new attitude about selling out.

A good buddy of mine in New York is a major television commercial producer. He proudly boasts a clientele that reads like a who's who from *Fortune Magazine*. You'd think he would be a multimillionaire with all those firms under his belt. In fact, he's barely making it and almost went bankrupt a few years ago.

He has Proposal Fever.

His problem became clear to me and my associates one day when we waded through the papers in his office. There were pages and notes of extremely good ideas everywhere, any single one worth thousands, if developed.

But he was so enamored with the romance and excitement of the idea phase that he mailed his thoughts to every prospect he could think of. Very often, he would ask for nothing in return and often didn't even bother to follow-up on these great ideas.

Did corporations use his proposals and ideas? Very often. Did he get paid or even recognized for these ideas? Not usually. He never learned to protect himself contractually and never learned the mechanics of the follow-up phases.

You don't have to be a non-professional to unwittingly give away all of your hard work. People at all levels get short-changed on their ideas to the tune of billions of dollars daily. Why do you think so many lawyers get rich? They rake it in from the simple mistakes you and I make.

Believe it or not, lawyers and good advice can become your best allies if used before the crisis erupts. A lot of you are afraid to pursue your great idea past the thrill of the romance stage. Seeing your concept at the model phase is primarily gratifying for your ego but serves little other purpose toward your goal of marketing, control and profit.

A lot of my new clients come to me as bitter people, convinced that advertising and success only happen to the other

27

guy. So they hire me and pay my hefty fees because they've either given up on their own talents or they haven't read this book.

People become bitter when they try it the wrong way and then refuse to learn the right way. They become convinced that their way proves that the system doesn't work for them. If they had done it right, maybe I'd be out of a job but they would be happier people. There's nothing like participating in a success but you must have incentive.

Much of my work involves keeping people excited by showing them the fruits of their efforts at each step. One should never underestimate the power of instilling incentive and confidence.

Lee Iacocca's incentive plans for Chrysler were so good, they were actually greater than he was. Against his wishes, a strike in late 1985 was settled by paying his workers fees that gave them parity with competitive autoworkers. Iacocca was not terribly keen on the idea. He thought it would drain the company dry.

The strikers won and a month after settlement, the company posted some of their strongest earnings ever. His own philosophy of incentive triumphed. That which is perceived as an "Ultra-Incentive" will produce Ultra-results.

You will always keep your incentive in your pursuits because you will always create for yourself the proper involvement at each step. Never sell out unless you're talking fortunes and retirement, even then, it's nice to keep a hand in just in case you need the production resources.

In fact, you are going to learn to have more than just an interest. Your prospects and associates will realize that you are uniquely qualifed to merit a controlling and supervisory interest. After all, it's your baby.

Your first premise is to never use the dime-store approach when selling your product. The dime-store approach implies taking a flat fee for a product or idea then just walking away. You're paid a fee that may seem sizeable to you and then you go home and wash your hands of the whole thing. The idea that has been so much a part of you and so important to you and now you're just going to cash out.

You've turned your dream into something that someone will buy from you. Sometimes the first-time thrill of that idea makes people lose their perspective.

An extremely persnickety client of mine gave birth to one of the first miniature home air-filtration systems. He was a scientist and knew very little about marketing. He sold out and then watched helplessly as his invention was picked apart, cheapened and rendered almost inoperative.

This bastardization of his brain-child nearly drove him crazy. This was his product. Subsequently, he marched into the bank, mortgaged his two homes to the hilt and bought back full rights to his products.

He redeveloped it and got it to market his way. After he had broken even and was well on his way to enjoying a tremendous bonanza, imitations began popping up all over the place, developed and distributed by major companies worldwide.

By the time he came to me, all the major producers and distributors were well on their way to burying him alive. He blew it by selling out in the first place so when it came time to legitimately utilize the services of a distributor, he refused to trust anyone but himself.

By not maintaining proper control, he had ultimately rendered his efforts obsolete.

I'm sure I could have helped him if he had come to me earlier but when he finally did come to me, his only options were either to sell the company before it went bankrupt or to develop an entirely new idea.

He streamlined his company and went back to the drawing board. He'll be back smarter and stronger, I hope.

The final decision is yours. If you want to just take the money and run, I can't stop you but obviously I don't advise it unless we're talking big bucks. Even then, as with the situation I just described, selling out may not be your best option.

What you have learned thus far has helped you to get started but it's only the beginning. You're still caught in the thrill of a brand-new romance. Now comes the marriage.

You've brought your idea closer to perfection and now you just can't wait to go back to those grand rounds and show up your critics. You probably think that my next piece of advice is to make just such a presentation. You couldn't be more wrong.

You began with an idea and then you turned the abstract into something tangible, a product or service, at least twice critiqued and refined at this point. You started as a shaky dreamer. Then I made you a researcher, an inventor, a designer, a developer. That's quite a company you're becoming.

We've worked hard to increase the value of you and your company. You may indeed go back to a manufacturer or distributor and work with them. You'll have to ultimately make the best determination for you and your venture. After this chapter, your options should clarify.

If you're thinking of becoming a "sell-out," be aware that many ideas are purchased and are then never released. Companies often buy out competitive ideas just to crush any potential competition. So if you do sell out, get a production commitment to insure your profit.

Or, as you have already observed, many ideas die from a simple case of misdirection. The bottom line is; don't let your good ideas die for any price. The world always needs better ways to do things. Your idea could make a difference.

So where do you go from here? How about to the marketplace. That's right, you read it right. All you have is a rough, refined prototype. You have nothing in production yet I am going to expose you to the marketplace.

You are about to undergo what is commonly known as a market test. You've gotten samples in the mail of new products. That kind of promotion can cost millions and what if the product has to be modified? The cheapest market surveys can cost thousands of dollars even before you know if your product is ready.

You don't want to spend that kind of money on your project. But would you be willing to invest under ten dollars plus a little time to test your idea?

Remember Hitchcock. We have to find out how the public and related industries feel about what we're up to. We have our legal protection and research behind us. Let's find out what the world is theeenking.

You may already have a distributor and/or manufacturer in mind. Wouldn't it be simple just to build that relationship and move ahead. Be advised, there may be several people out there who can help your product come to life. Don't limit yourself to one chance prospect.

Here's your assignment; Write three paragraphs describing the features and benefits of your idea. Is it new? Say so and explain what it does that may render existing competitors obsolete. Don't explain how. Don't be too technical and don't give away too many hints about your research conclusions. And, by all means, always include at least a mailing address and preferably a phone number.

Convey that your product is available for distribution or participation (if appropriate). This is done to officiate and lend credibility to your product or service. DO NOT EVER lie about your product. Genuine advertising is a responsibility to the public to tell the truth in an attractive and appealing manner.

I'm sure you have noticed that some of the most outrageous claims are made for some of the most inferior products. The harder someone tries to sell something to me, the more dubious I become. Don't promise magic, just better features and benefits than the other guy.

Write something that you would believe, yourself. If necessary, utilize the writing techniques I described in

Chapter 3. Run it by some friends. We're not looking for cute copy, "just the facts, mam."

Is your writing understandable? Can people get an idea of what your product is about just from your paragraphs? Have you created curiosity?

Spend a week writing if you need to but no more than that. Don't get stuck. I write these types of descriptions all of the time and my blurbs appear in hundreds of magazines each year. Since I have been doing them for almost fifteen years, I can usually churn them out in less than an hour. Ultimately, you'll be able to do the same thing. You should be able to write as fast as you can clearly relate your ideas in ordinary conversation.

Congratulations! You have just produced your first press release. Now the trick is to get the message to the right people. This book is laced with the common theme of bringing each task to a successful conclusion. This is both exhilarating and terrifying for many of you who never dreamed they would ever see anything of theirs in print. But you'll soon discover how easy it can be.

Nothing is easy until you master it but if you've made it this far, you can make it the rest of the way. Many of you don't believe it and I used to lose a lot of promising students at this stage. It's easy to get stuck right before your big debut. I have found it necessary to throw in the next very brief chapter. After, you've read it, I expect you to have no excuses for not moving ahead.

Chapter 5

DON'T GET STUCK
There's Always A Way

Ideas die when people don't know what to do next to move them forward. It happens all the time. Ignorance and lack of confidence are the leading cause of death among promising ventures. Even business professionals can be afraid to admit that certain delays are caused by procedural ignorance so all you hear from them are excuses and stories. Pride or fear of job security shields ignorance and the idea falls victim.

Good business health is determined by any measurable signs of moving forward. Even when struggling, people who dedicate themselves to making their product move ahead are rarely depressed.

Keep it going. If you don't know, ask, learn. If you have a problem, solve it. There's always an economical, ethical and effective way.

As I was putting this book together, some of my critics told me to cut any words of encouragement and just stick to the "How To Stuff." This was one time when I found my critics to be dead wrong. The world is full of "How To" Encyclopedias on how to do anything, but with little sympathy for how you, the reader, is thinking. So instead of learning "How To" with many of these books, you learn "How NOT To" once you run up against your first inhuman directive that you don't understand.

You learn how not to permanently by creating fear and lack of confidence as your biggest enemies. Your venture success is a highly personal issue and I want no one to be left behind.

I can't get too heavy and I can't play psychologist. All I can say is that, if you're stuck, there's always a way to get unstuck. Find it.

To those of you who are now ready to move forward, go get em! You're going to encounter a lot of characters who might try to raise your blood pressure and steal your sleep and worse. My intention is to not have you lose a single night's sleep.

You see, it doesn't make any difference what kind of characters approach you, I'll teach you how to deal with them. You'll have the control and the upper hand. If anyone loses sleep, it'll be the other guy, not you.

Fear no one. This is your game and you make the final rules.

Alas, there is still a segment of you who have never finished a "How To" Book or any venture, for that matter. You began with the best of intentions and hopes but then repeated the same old pattern of fear and failure, like a worm crawling around the inside of a cup, round and around until it dies.

Maybe you have spent years training yourself not to succeed and therefore have never had a success past a certain level. You now will have the know-how to break that cycle. Know that you've got it, believe that you've got it and go for it.

America can be a very exciting place because it attempts to encourage free thought and this type of environment is most conducive to heightened productivity. If you allow yourself to be left behind, you deprive all of us.

In the next chapter, we really begin dealing with all of the shenanigans of the product and promotion game. I'll give you the best idea possible as to what to expect but life is always full of surprises. Just remember to keep moving forward.

Chapter 6

EVALUATING MARKETING RESPONSE
Hello Out There. What Do You Think?

It was frustrating in the beginning when I told you not to bother your friends at parties. You wanted to brag about this spectacular romance you were having with an idea.

Think back at what a shabby state your idea was in back then. What would your friends and associates have thought of you if that spark fizzled out. Now you are ready to profit from a little showing off. You've made it this far and you're going all the way. It's time for them to bother you at the party.

We begin by taking that literary work of art you created and getting it published. Call two local newspapers and tell them what you're up to. "Local Boy Makes Good." Every paper has a space for that kind of material. Send them or if possible, present in person your paragraphs about your widget. But NO PICTURES, PLEASE! Of you or especially of your product. All you're aiming to do with these P.R. annoucements is to create curiosity. This valuable publicity should not cost you one red cent to run in your local papers.

There's no reason to worry whether your writing is good enough for the paper. If they need to, they'll perfect for you, free of charge. Then you'll have professional copy to adapt for future use.

Plan these few releases in the papers at one-week intervals. Locate a local magazine and see if you can arrange publication of your release. If you know of a local trade magazine relevant to your idea then send your copy to them.

Otherwise, just one or two local neighborhood or regional magazines will work just fine. We'll learn how to utilize those trade magazines in upcoming chapters.

Not every publication will accommodate your needs but many will. The magazine releases should appear about three to five weeks after your newspaper releases. That will give you more rewrite time, if needed. And remember, no pictures.

What about radio or TV. Is there a local radio station or two that your friends listen to? Radio stations have spots called P.S.A.'s (Public Service Announcements). If your product is in any way a community service, you can usually get a couple of these public service announcements read on the air for free. Try it.

Cable TV is giving the small towns a stronger voice with regards to local media happenings. I'm not asking you to put your face on TV yet but a lot of these small town cable stations have TV bulletin boards. Get your announcement on TV if applicable.

Don't sit by the phone expecting miracles to happen. Some of you may get two responses. Some of you may get twenty. Be patient. This is feedback and refinement time.

Okay, you have gotten your initial P.R. going and your releases will all be appearing within the next month or two. I am hoping you'll receive just a small handful of credible inquiries. You should correspond or preferably meet face to face with at least five inquiries.

Why did they respond to your announcement? Find out what their specific interest might be in your gem. Build a file of each contact and their talents. Don't eliminate anyone as a possible participant at some future date unless they are dishonest or are simply trying to make money off of you.

All these people should be teaching you how to perfect your product. With every productive meeting, your product should improve, as will your own value as an authority.

It's a good thing you held out through this chapter

because this is when the big business breakthroughs begin to happen. Many of you will clearly see how to move ahead with all the energy in the world.

Many of you will actually get offers of employment or capital to make your product go.

If these releases don't catapult you into stardom, that's perfectly all right. The point is you have learned to develop a good idea without selling out or losing your shirt. Depending on your situation, you have saved anywhere from several hundred dollars to several thousand dollars.

After a few weeks or months, you may want to repeat this P.R. query process. To get a release in the exact same periodical, announce a new development in your work. Do not do more than two of these preliminary release programs because we want to get on to our production phase. Chapters 9 and 10 will further explore all components of the P.R. issue.

Now you can throw a party. Invite your friends as well as some of the new business contacts you made to celebrate the birth of your idea. The party should help create momentum and support. In a positive social environment where people are feeling their best, you'll get some very good advice and feedback. Just be dutiful about following up on the promises people make. That's your only way of finding out if the promises are real or not.

Let the ideas flow. If your product requires any degree of assembly, you are looking for those components. For first-timers, I have two bits of advice about componenture.

The first is: Beware of the high cost of buying too cheaply. Why buy sub-standard or lower quality parts that could destroy your entire project, not to mention your business credibility. Components like that aren't a bargain at any price.

Whenever I trade stories with electronics marketers, we always seem to have a new battery-story to laugh about. When first-timers have a product that requires pre-installation of household-type batteries, they almost invariably head across the border or overseas where they buy batteries for next to nothing. These foreign specials generally last just until the consumer gets the failed product. After all recalls for replacement with quaility batteries plus repair of damage from their leaking predecessors, it's a bit difficult to view those cheap batteries as any kind of bargain.

So buy quality and secondly make every effort to buy American. If price is your problem here, negotiate. It's always better to keep it all here where you can have control.

You've heard though that your basic assembly labor costs are much lower overseas but added to your overseas costs are the costs of shipping, insurance, etc. And international patent protection from such assembly plants is a real nightmare.

There are many able labor/assembly outlets throughout the U.S. whose owners want to work out a cost-effective arrangement. Give them a chance.

If your product requires simple assembly, why not consider the mentally retarded or other disabled or institutionalized people who could do an excellent job for similar costs?

If your product is more sophisticated, explore various senior citizens or veterans organizations before you go trading overseas. And what about a local trade or business school?

Take advantage of your Yankee Ingenuity before you rob America of even a single job. You'll be more than just pleasantly surprised, your efforts could make you a community hero. This vital element for product success is further explained in Chapters 9 and 10.

So for now, you have this wealth of knowledge and excitement that you have generated. How far you have come, yet don't be tempted to rest on a gratified ego. You can play those games after you succeed otherwise you'll kill your progress.

You must organize all this data to give you fuel for progress. A danger point here is weak follow-up. Keep a planning calendar handy and be responsible about all your prospects.

Keep your development meetings to the point and don't let them stray. This is a time for good ideas and not for rambling. There's a great difference between activity and accomplishment. Think results.

Chapter 7

PRODUCTION PLANNING
Moving Ahead With Interest

Some of your respondents to your P.R. may be from some of the contacts you made in your initial research phase. That can prove to be a very encouraging development.

Last time you encountered these experts, you were just a babe in the woods and they were the authorities. If you did your homework properly, the tables have now turned. Your efforts have elevated your value to your potential associates.

Hear these prospects out but make no promises. Ideally, you'll want to entertain many possibilities before creating any type of written agreement. I'm going to present a host of your basic options and then you can decide what best suits you. Whatever you do, sign nothing, agree to nothing until a competent attorney reviews any and all proposals.

Some of you honestly feel that you have gone as far as you can on development and production planning. The nature of your product requires a specific manufacturing technology to move ahead. It may indeed be the correct time to explore potential associates.

If this is the right time to approach the heavies, let's do it right. I want you to be well protected. Arrange a meeting with the company's decision-maker(s) so you won't have to duplicate efforts or waste time with a go-between who could distort the hard information.

Be very open. Find out exactly what they want to do with your product and what they are willing to offer you. Remember, you are never to sell out completely. After all, as an expert on your product, your services could be of great value to them. If your prospects are smart, they will realize that they need you as much as your creation.

Inform your prospects that you feel it would be to their benefit if you stayed with the project through all stages. After you finish this book, you will find that you really can be of great value to them in many key areas.

You may consider suggesting to these serious prospects that your compensation be in the form of a modest monthly consulting fee plus a percentage of the gross profits that your product generates. This type of option can prove highly appealing to a company who originally had thought they were going to have to pay you a small fortune up front. The way I have suggested represents a better risk for all parties concerned.

A business deal is not a good one unless it benefits all participants involved. Some of you may indeed require the services of a major distributor but may not need the manufacturing end. Consider the following:

Several years ago, I did the advertising for several pool and spa product companies. They made all the pool fittings, drains, skimmers, etc.

One day as a favor to the boss, I made a delivery of prototypes to an injection-molding company. When I got there, I couldn't believe what I saw. It was my first time visiting a plastic molder. Here lie the deepest darkest secrets of virtually all the major competitors. This is where virtually all these different companies had their plastic pool components made, all by this one little company.

How could one company claim to be more special than the next? Anyone could stroll into that plastics company and have their product made and "Bingo" they're in business.

It was really almost that simple and I actually know people who broke off from a parent pool company and began their own successful enterprise this way. Of course, I should also add that they used my advertising techniques to really get an edge.

Don't worry, you'll learn all about my special promotional techniques in upcoming chapters. My only point with the great pool product caper is that you should not rush to give your product and profits to a big company who might end up using the same manufacturing company you would use.

Suppose you're planning to start up a small hometown paper. You could go to a local publisher who could essentially take it over. Or you could find a printer with periodical printing experience. No matter what you've got, if you attempt to line up your "jobbers," you can reduce your dependency on any type of parent operation.

In pre-production, aside from protection, there is one other key element that cannot be ignored nor overlooked. A lot of inventors are very rebellious and then there are many of you who are strict conformists. The nature of your concepts could be as different as night and day but in the area of state and/or federal regulations, safety standards or any other mandatory codes or laws regarding safety and approval of your goods or service, there are no shortcuts. And if you think you know one, forget it.

Safety standards and the like are in place to protect all of us. Adhere to them like Krazy Glue. Determine if you need certain safety, and/or other approvals and take proper steps to get them.

Have you ever bought a new screwdriver at a flea market only to find that it chipped away after its first use? What if a fragment caught in your eye. What kind of bargain is that? There are millions of such stories with much worse consequences. A bargain is a quailty item at a lower price, not a substandard product that looks like a steal.

If you're out to make a quick buck and you have any intention of taking safety shortcuts, I despise you. You pose a real danger to the safety of my family and anyone else you deceive into buying your product. Enough said.

As a result of your P.R. campaign, money may seem to fall from the sky. Some of you have been approached by people who want to help fund your efforts. These types fall into two basic categories: The first is one who will give you a sizeable amount of capital, essentially as a loan secured by your product.

That kind of offer can tempt a lot of us but it's just plain foolish to take on a loan burden at this stage of the game.

You could also be approached by the venture capitalist. This person may advance you a certain amount of money for the development of your product. You will pay him back by pledging to this person a modest percentage of your net profits for a specific amount of time.

The major rule I have about money offers is: Don't take it unless you legitimately need it for your venture. Two times in my life, I actually turned down venture capital. Once at age 23, I had a small folk record company called "Warped Records & Tapes, Inc." I had invested twelve hundred dollars into this venture. After production of our second record, I was offered fifty thousand dollars in exchange for half interest in my company by a major stockbroker. Maybe I was overwhelmed, maybe I didn't believe it could happen to me. I turned the money down and Warped Records maintained its "nonprofit" status.

Another time I was offered seventy-five thousand dollars from a client of mine. He said the money was mine to play with if I could just present to him an idea good enough to invest the money in. I felt like a 13 year-old virgin being raped by a Playboy Bunny. Me, the guy who was always creative, suddenly was without a thought in my head. I couldn't think of anything and he subsequently invested the money elsewhere.

Money by itself at the wrong time doesn't always spell opportunity. Unfortunately, I wasn't ready for these two great opportunities. But both of these people are still very good friends of mine. Imagine what would have happened if I had taken the money with no real plan in mind.

Don't worry. There are many other times when I did utilize such money sources but with a solid plan behind me. I've always preferred to keep my friends instead of trying to take the money and run.

Even with the absolute best of intentions, you are going to run into situations that may shock your sensibilities to the core. Broken promises, broken contracts, snake oil, the lessons come hard and fast. As long as you keep your sense of humor you can persist and prevail.

Each chapter has represented specific missions for you to focus upon and achieve. You've come this far so you know your idea is a feasible one. A wonderful elderly Mexican friend of mine always used to say, "Poco a poco, caminos lejos." Translation: "Little by little, we walk far."

So keep walking and protect yourself by protecting your interest in your creation. America was built on productivity and productivity makes money, not the other way around.

You have now gotten your product to the genuine pre-production stage. You have either married a company or you have ventured out on your own. In either case, we have just barely begun to make things happen.

Something you made, created, some concept you introduced is ready to happen on a level where it could prove profitable. You're excited and you're already picking out the color of your Rolls Royce. Or your associated company, usually small, is hopeful that your product is going to work out.

What do you do? Do you make thousands of 'em, Millions? "Why not!" you think. Everything's ready to go. You and/or your developers have worked all the bugs out and everyone seems to be suggesting "Full Speed Ahead."

Even if that's what your manufacturing associates or whoever are suggesting, present them with this premise and option. Premise: All parties with a vested interest want your idea to bear fruit as soon as possible so that a healthy road to profit can be realized. Of course! Well if your associates agree with this premise then you should propose the following option: In that no one wants the road to profit interrupted once full-fledged sales begin, you need to do one final test.

Your associates may be somewhat annoyed at your insolence and suggestion of any delay at this point. You've already run a P.R. reaction test. You and maybe some technicians have tried to anticipate each and every pitfall.

You never know how your users are really going to react once they start using your product. Up to now, all of our tests and theories are only models that may anticipate what consumer reaction will be. Even some consumers have told you they know the idea is going to be a hit.

Will they say the same thing after they've actually used and worked with your product? No guarantees. One final test may save you a lot of problems down the road. If I am representing a new product, I attempt to give away twenty to one hundred of the product before I release it for actual sale. With high-tech products, your budget may limit you from doing this. Even if you can get a few out in a good public field test, the benefits could save you a small fortune down the road.

Some pre-market tests involve thousands of give-aways or test-sales in various geographical areas. The majority of you will not need to go through such extremes.

I first arrived in California as a young country bumpkin with limited agency experience. My only agency background was as a copywriter for the American Express radio account under Ogilvy & Mather Advertising, Inc. in New York.

Once in California, with my reasonable degree of courage and some intelligence, I was destined to glean a very rapid education.

In L.A., my first boss was a very nice person who dressed well and meant well but had not one inkling about how to create an ad. On my very first day, I was presented with an immediate problem. My new agency could not figure out why a certain account was so displeased with them. They had expended a lot of energy on the client's product, one of the first remote switches.

I was shown a magazine ad which they said produced no results. One glance at the ad and I was ready to wow them with my great advertising abilities.

The ad displayed a gorgeous color photo with two people in their backyard spa, below which was a headline which read as follows:

"....Presenting the Ultimate In Convenience"

Just what the public was looking for, the ultimate INCONVENIENCE. What an embarrassment. And when they told me the ad was already in print, I would have quit that first day if I wasn't starving to death.

The time to make your mistakes is backstage i.e. my testing phases. Relatively private screw-ups are nothing compared to the same hunk of stupidity times a thousand or a million. Protect yourself. And take chances? Absolutely. You gain nothing if you take no chances but concurrently, you'll make no progress if you don't protect each step.

You've heard the expression, "Worst Case Scenario." What if wayward finances turn your best friend into your worst enemy? What if you're sloppy about the testing phases? Who's liable? You? Your affiliates? Plan and aim for success but don't let your anxieties stop you from protecting yourself. And keep up that friendly relationship with your attorney. You can haggle most of the details but your attorney can often very quickly insure that you made the agreement you thought you made.

Building good solid business friends can make a real difference. If your concept doesn't quite work out as planned the first time, don't write off some of your original associates. If they like the way you have presented yourself and your ideas they may well be apt to try it again with you.

After all, who is going to know more about what steps not to take than you.

So let's see how well you can observe, anticipate and correct mistakes. Give your product or service to some average users for no charge, if possible. Let them play with it and run it through the mill for a few weeks, or longer, if necessary.

Encourage your subjects to be ruthless and excessive but not dangerous. Then go back to them and beg for their worst, meanest criticism of your product. If they love it and have nothing rotten to say, persist until they come up with something good and negative.

Make certain you are in the proper frame of mind. Listen carefully to what your test market has to say. Write or record this feedback and thank your subjects. Do not argue with them. Even though your concept may be very dear to you, just throw your pride out the window for now. Then go home and decipher the valid from the far-fetched. If you evaluate your data correctly, your pride will prevail in the end.

If necessary, retrieve all of your products and bring them back to the drawing board.

If you had, say a hundred random test subjects and their responses were generally and genuinely favorable, that can be interpreted as a very healthy sign. If some of your subjects almost fight you and refuse to give it back, that's an even better sign, as you'll see in the next chapter.

If you got a lot of tomatoes in your face, fine. Go back and patiently make those changes. Then take a moment to thank your lucky stars that you have saved all interested parties from a devastating recall or worse. If ever you could tastefully recite the phrase, "An ounce of prevention is worth a pound of cure," and sound convincing, this has to be that time.

This chapter may have saved you ten dollars or ten million. This book is becoming a better bargain all the time.

Chapter 8

PRICING, SALES AND DISTRIBUTION
How To Face "How-to-aphobia"

For those of you with some sales background, this is an excellent period for you. You can finally ply your trade with more product knowledge and enthusiasm than you have ever had.

A lot of you, however are chronic Sales Howtoaphobics. You're not just afraid of sales, you're twice as fearful about believing any advice regarding how you can become an able salesperson.

Pricing, sales and distribution are highly complex areas and there are thousands of books dealing with these areas in particular. The only intention of this chapter is to make it relevant to your venture. Through this chapter, you'll get enough of a briefing to get things headed toward the results you need.

Much to your surprise, I am not going to cure you with a host of appropriate platitudes (though a few good ones come to mind). You can read every good authority and get a million good ideas. The real trick is to make it all relate to your venture.

Up til now, no book has ever proven to you that you can actually put all that good advice to work for you. If only one of these references could prove to you that you really can sell, then you would have the sufficient reinforcement to make sales happen.

Finally, you have invested in a book that's going to have you prove to yourself once and for all that you can sell, no matter what your background or fears.

It wasn't very difficult for most of you to engage those test subjects in the last chapter. Did any of them really love your product or in fact express an interest in buying one? Very nice, you just made your first sale and it didn't hurt a bit.

Some of your test subjects have suggested refinements. Now that you have made those refinements, those subjects could also get very interested in your improved version. After all, you have improved life somehow with your idea. Everybody wants improvement in their day-to-day lives.

From the simplest, most direct and most important level of sales, person to person, your final testing phase has given you more sales experience than you ever realized. Your testers have worked hard for you and now they want to buy the perfected version. To show your gratitude for their help, you will sell it to them at a greatly discounted price.

Price!? What about price. How do you know what to charge for your goodies? There are a few givens. In theory, merchandise must be competitively priced as perceived by the customer, but you also must make a profit.

Wait a minute! There are excellent pens for well under a dollar and there are pens priced at several hundred dollars. Therefore, competitive pricing also refers to the class of the product.

Our ears ring daily from the barrage of special value sales that in essence suggest, "Get the same quality at a lower price."

The following client wished to remain anonymous. You'll soon see why. After several years of a mutually profitable relationship, he informed me one day that he no longer needed my marketing and advertising services. He was a "slow-pay" client so I was somewhat relieved at losing the account.

Three years later, a former associate of mine sent me a clipping. My old pal had gone bankrupt. Though I was certainly sorry to hear of his losses, I had to confess to an inward pleasure of seeing the consequences of the absence of my services.

I decided to call him to find out what happened. I knew his products were some of the finest on the market but the competition was creeping in. Without any marketing expertise, all he knew how to do was lower his prices, which finally got so low, his business collapsed.

Believe me, quality wars are better than price wars. Your efforts thus far should permit you to be competitive if your product represents a realistic improvement. Price wars can cheapen the public's image of your product and then wipe you out.

But there's a lot more involved in the pricing process than the mere comparison of a final selling (retail) price. Somehow, you have to eventually absorb all start-up and research costs. A competent tax accountant will help you to realize any legitimate deductions for your efforts, as well as all tax obligations.

After deductions, you must determine what your actual expenditures are. From inception to production, you can't miss a penny. And it doesn't stop there. What about shipping, distribution, advertising? Who pays for it all?

Every step right up to the final consumer shaves a little of your profit away. Still, there are ways to keep those costs down to a bare minimum. The adage of cutting out the middleman is more gimmicry than anything else. You may need legitimate middlemen to insure that your product sells on a large scale.

I had previously suggested that you could consider controlling the manufacture of your idea. If you have done that, you can now potentially earn a bigger piece of the pie for your efforts.

Instead of approaching a manufacturer, you could make a similar deal with a competent distributor, although there are excellent ways to begin as your own distributor, as you will soon see.

Unless born from a merger of two monsters, most businesses began as small mom and pop garage ventures. Distribution may have meant driving around in the old jalopy and dropping off the goods at a few households for a certain retail price which, for this example we'll set at $5.00 per item.

Then a couple of local little stores wanted to buy the product. Our little manufacturer/distributor sells his product to them at the wholesale price of $2.50.

In time, hundreds of stores want to sell this product, far more than the jalopy can cover. Enter the distributor who buys each item for $2.00 and then distributes it to the stores for the wholesale cost of $2.50

How do you connect with all these distributors and retailers? I'm proud to say that I discover new ways every day.

In fact, if admission of ignorance is the first step towards wisdom, then I guess you'd have to say that brokering officially licensed products from the '84 Olympics made me and my associates very wise. Much of this account was a heavily intensified and rushed education about every aspect of product development and sales.

My favorite part of that entire period were the trade shows and conventions. That was where everyone really got the chance to ply their trade. The salespeople sold at their best, the buyers bought, often more than planned due to the excitement of it all. And ideas flutter back and forth like the swallows changing direction at Capistrano.

I had represented scores of products at many shows before the Olympics but never such a diversity in such a short time. If you have never been to a convention, trade show or seminar in your field of endeavor, you're really missing something.

If feasible try to introduce your product or service, or at least attend a relevant trade show, carnival, flea market or fair. These can all be excellent avenues for building your sales knowledge and confidence.

You can pick so much valuable sales, pricing and distribution data during a day or two at the right event. Generally, all the heavies in your field will be there and you can see just where you and your product stand.

Of greater interest is that you could make some great sales at the right event. Two warnings: In all the excitement, you'll hear a lot of empty promises. Try to sort them out then find and cash in on those few real leads. Secondly, to make this financially feasible, we are looking for broad-scale success. One show is just a speck in your overall sales plan.

Some of you are planning to open-up a specialty retail store to sell your product directly to the public. That's a good and sensible way to start if you can muster the capital. You may however, want to first try out your wares in an already existing store, if feasible.

There are as many ways to get your goods or services to market as there are products. Throughout this manual, we have explored the most cost-effective means to achieve our successes. What I am going to show you next is such a powerful tool that, if all of you use it correctly, conventional advertising will never and should never be the same. That's the American way.

So good luck. I hope you put me out of a job.

Chapter 9

CREDIBLE, ALMOST-FREE ADVERTISING THAT WORKS
"Hey boss, look at this"

Advertising. Madison Avenue. Those creative geniuses who have the power to make you buy or do anything.

There seems to be a buyer (market) for everything and anything. All you have to do is find it and influence it. We are told that obnoxious, repetitive TV commercials actually make us remember to buy those products. Are we really all that stupid or is what we generally see as advertising simply the best we are capable of?

As an advertising professional (or person, depending on your point of view), I watch the TV commercials more than I watch conventional shows. It's like watching twelve little shows every half hour. Commercials seem to be getting more glitzy and creative all the time. But is the increasingly shrewd American consumer really buying all this new vaudeville?

Am I looking for reflections of trends? Not especially. Technique? Very often. And do I believe the claims I see? Very very rarely. In fact, the TV is my lantern looking for an honest commercial.

Credibility. That's what you're after. How can you ever really be sure that people who buy their own commercials are telling you the unbiased truth? Some present what they call hard facts and statistics only to be rebutted by a competitor's contradictory facts.

Very often, paid ads lie and that seems to be acceptable because people have traditionally responded by purchasing those goods or services.

So where do I find my trends? I watch and read the news, everything I can get a hold of. I don't believe what people or ads tell me unless I can really prove it. Try this: Go out and buy one of my favorite magazines, *Consumer Reports*.

Pick out a couple of products that you believe to be the best available and then see what *Consumer Reports* has to say about it. Generally, you'll be surprised and disappointed.

The credibility factor. You were fooled by conventional advertising.

I became aware of this con-job several years ago and it really bothered me. "Deeze Dem Doze" clients would throw me a chunk of money, as if it were a dog bone and say, "Buy me an ad in dis here magazine." (Generally referring to the magazine of their trade.) I made a healthy profit and they would see themselves in the magazine. The only problem was I wasn't giving them the credibility they needed.

If an advertising agency has already tried to get their hooks into you, they have most likely told you that paid advertising is the only way to succeed. Since selling and producing ads is probably the only way they can stay in business, what on earth else are they going to tell you?

Well now you know differently. First of all, you have a leg up on most ad agencies because of the mountains of research you have already carried out.

Research and homework are where any real advertising campaign actually begin. Ironically enough, it is often the weakest area for agencies. They'll give you a ton of ideas on how to spend your money but not much actual research.

That's why my "Deeze Dem Doze" clients get so mad. They spend a wad of money on a couple of ads against my recommendations and then they tell me advertising doesn't work.

Just because a salesman tells you to buy an ad doesn't

mean that you just bought a ticket to guaranteed success. Challenge those salesmen. How many of them would only take a fee only if their ads worked? Witness credibility succumbing to mere greed.

When I'm given a budget to make a product successful, I consider that money to be a loan that I aim to pay back tenfold. I spend very little of my client's money until I can make that client's business grow. A no-response ad campaign does more than make a client mad, it's a dream-killer and I have promised to protect your dreams.

Put those advertising agency and sales people on hold for now. Don't join the hundreds of thousands of people who waste billions on incorrect advertising procedures. If the masses want to keep wasting their money, that's their problem.

For your debut, I have a far more credible procedure that will cost you next to nothing. Most of you are more than half-way there already.

I have often asked audiences to guess how many magazines are printed in the world today. I hear numbers like a hundred or a few thousand but never the actual number which easily exceeds several hundred thousand. Name a topic, any topic whatsoever. There's a magazine that covers that subject. Ever heard of *Ballet News,* or *Bow and Arrow Monthly,* or *Totally Housewares*? How about *Poultry Digest Magazine* or *Plastics Business Magazine*?

America is not divided by cities and towns but by thousands of subcultures represented by magazines. Each month, over thirty thousand people read *Ballet News.* Over one hundred thousand read *Bow and Arrow* each month.

Any topic, no matter how bizarre or mundane, has a relevant magazine and a world of people whose livelihood is affected by it. Are you aware of the publications that pertain to your product? Here's how you find them.

For our purposes, we shall be looking at three categories of publications: 1) Newspapers, local and possibly, national. 2) Consumer magazines i.e. those geared to the public retail trade. 3) And finally the mighty trade, technical and professional magazines targeted to product manufacturing, distribution and all other pre-consumer areas.

Your assignment is to track down ten publications in each of the three categories if that many exist. The newspapers should just be your every day papers. For the consumer magazines, if possible, at least five should be relevant to your product's industry.

The other five require a little brainstorming on your part. They should be general or broad topic magazines where an audience for your product or service may be available. For example, if you've invented a pair of scissors, you may pick up a hardware journal or cutlery news but you should also pick up a magazine about paper products, textiles or maybe, school supplies. You're seeking out related industries.

Use the five and five rule for the trade technical or professional magazine category as well. Now, how do I know these publications exist and where the heck do you find them? The easiest place to start is at the manufacturers that you've dealt with. They'll generally have the trade magazines of your industry lying around somewhere.

If you can't hunt them down that way, there are some excellent reference books that list every publication you'll ever want to know about. If you know of a local ad agency, see if they will lend you these directory books for a few hours. If that is not possible, check your local library for any of the writer's market books.

My favorite source books are the Standard Rate and Data Service books out of Skokie, Illinois. They are expensive to buy but their data books list everything ever published.

For the publications you have picked, get copies of as many of them as possible. Take a few minutes to get familiar with each one. Especially in the trade mags, study the ads, some of which may one day be your competition.

How do manufacturers and distributors keep an eye on

the competition? There are many sophisticated ways. One way is to stay well read. Keeping an ongoing monitor on the market means all manufacturing costs and technological developments are up to date.

You could watch or read ads but you already know that ads aren't your most credible source of information. Let me tell you about a holiday that occurs at nearly every manufacturer or distributor just about every few weeks. It's called, "Hey boss, look-at-this" day.

On any given morning when the trade magazines arrive, the salespeople rush to grab a copy, of which there are generally several. Do they quickly skim through the ads? No. Do they sit down to read a nice long article? Not at this time.

You will see them turn to one place first and study it intently. That section is known as the "New Product," "Product News," "Industry News" or a number of other similar headings.

Their eyes feverishly scan this section looking for what the industry is up to, studying the competition. The moment they see something that may affect their own product line, they dash into the main man's office and say, "Hey Boss, look at this!"

After years of advertising and scores of accounts, I have seen more things happen from the New Product sections than any other area of advertising. Those who followed the procedure I've outlined in this chapter have loved the money I have saved for them while giving their product a chance to prove itself.

Everyone benefits from proper use of the media. That's what you're learning here. Your first big media lesson will be through the magic of these New Product sections. If you receive tremendous results from a particular magazine, that may be the place to go for future paid advertising.

Notice that I do not call our initial campaign a P.R. tactic. It is not. P.R. or public relations involves using the media to display civic concerns of an individual or organization. Proper public relations will play a very powerful role for your cause as you will see in the next chapter.

For now, we are going to promote your concept on a very wide and powerful scale for almost no money and certainly a savings of several thousand dollars in advertising expense. We can do this because the cost to run a blurb and photo on your product is generally zero, free, no money.

Though some magazines do charge a space fee for their New Product Sections, most do not. Those that do not charge a fee are the smart ones because they invite and encourage the growth and prosperity of the free enterprise system. They invest a pittance in giving this space and if that helps to make your product a success, it could pave the way for a mutually profitable relationship.

There's an even more significant reason that they should give you free press. The introduction of your product or service is news and it's their job to report the news.

For a magazine to run one or two releases over a few months for you is usually no problem. Any more than that for the same new product is taking unfair advantage of the media system.

Time to build our image and substance in the corporate world. To start, I would like you to go to your local budget printer and have some business letterhead put together. You should develop a simple logo from the printer's art books, and include your name, phone number and address.

Print one hundred envelopes, cards and letter stock. This whole process should cost between one and two hundred dollars. If you have become affiliated with a company, use their letterhead and have them print business cards with your name on them.

If you're stuck for a good name for your company, don't settle for anything sarcastic. Cute or clever names are fine as long as they clearly indicate what the business is all about and they must not offend. Otherwise, use your last name followed by the publicly known name of your product. Example: "Jones Fertilizer Company" or "Smiths Laser Engineering."

If you need a title under your name and your item is a product, consider using the following label: "Product Research and Development." If your enterprise is service oriented, try "Manager" for blue collar or "Program Director" if it's white collar in nature.

If you think you can get away without using letterhead remember you will already be saving several grand in advertising costs. From an established image and credibility standpoint, get that letterhead, even if you can only afford fifty pieces.

To take the next steps for both my goods and service readers, we are going to create two fictional businesses. We'll call the first one "Women's Work, Inc." Two young women, one a single mother with no educational background and the other, a two-year business student with a knack for successfully starting small businesses, have formed a management company to help young women begin their own businesses.

We'll call our product company "Adams Reliable Auto Products" (Inc. if applicable). Retired chemist Fred Adams has developed a substance that not only cleans windshields, it removes scratches off the glass. During his little product debut party, a friend suggested he call his formula, "Windshield Swiper." The name stuck.

The first step for both companies is to take a photo. It must be a professional looking shot so if you can't do a proper job, find a professional who will do it for no more than twenty or thirty dollars. This is when it pays to have a friend who is a photo buff who can take an excellent photo for no charge.

To photograph Windshield Swiper, Mr. Adams had his local artist friend make up some labels and attached them to a couple of dummy bottles. He took a two-foot by three-foot sheet of clear white art paper. Since the bottles are a little dark, the white background will help to show up the product.

His photographer curved the art paper against a corner of the wall and floor to create what is called a seamless background. When the photo is processed, all the viewer sees is the product on a white background.

If Mr. Adams wanted to get a little more sophisticated he could also take a picture of his product in action, perhaps showing half of a scratch removed. Some products mandate a demonstration photo to make their function clear to the reader. Another advantage of the "Action Photo" is that it can get the message across more immediately.

For the Women's Work Company, the two women are currently working out of their own homes. Also it's harder to take a photo of their product. However, through their initial query releases, they already have one small client who has a very modern-looking office.

They don't know any photographers but they found an easy way around that one. One of the local papers has assigned a photographer to take a picture of them in their client's office. He has agreed to give them the full use of this excellent photo if they will promise to keep him in mind if ever they produce a major ad for a client or themselves.

Get the picture? You want a 3″ x 5″ glossy photo that the publications may enlarge or decrease. Generally your release will entail a few inches in a single column. But sometimes, you'll luck out and get much more space.

You need thirty clear copies, or the magazines won't run them. The least expensive copies are attainable at any photo-reproduction service who can make copies much cheaper than a photographer can. We are aiming to save money but we never want to look sloppy or disorganized.

Next we need to tell our readers what we're talking about. Dig out those original releases you submitted during your initial test phase. I assume they are in the form of a newspaper or magazine clipping. You can see that the various publications have usually modified and cleaned up your original literary gem.

Read the press releases in your collection of trade magazines. Get an idea of their style and layout. Get out your pen or tape recorder and rehash that release. Our fictional Mr. Adams has chosen his action photo to work with. Though he received some positive feedback from his original releases, he wasn't very pleased with how they were rewritten by the publications. Here's what they did:

"Adams Reliable Auto Products, Inc. of Worcester, MA, claims to have developed a product that supposedly removed scratches from windshields. For further information, write Adams Reliable Auto Products, P.O. Box 75, Worcester, MA."

"Claims?" "Supposedly?" What kind of help is that? The first time, most publications gave him only a couple of inches of space, at most. This time around, his releases are playing much better. Here's how most of them now read:

"Adams Reliable Auto Products, Inc. of Worcester, MA, introduces their new Windshield Cleaner/Scratch Remover. As seen in the photo, the product, called WIND-SHIELD SWIPER is one of the first ever to completely remove deep windshield scratches. After the scratch is removed, the glass is left completely clear and in tact. For further information, circle #85 on the reader-response card, or write Adams Reliable Auto Products, Inc., Box 75, Worcester, MA or call.... (include phone number!)."

He did five things differently this time. First, he sent a photo. Then he learned how to sharpen his description of Windshield Swiper. Then how did he get the magazine to eliminate the cynical wording? Very simple. He sent them a professional sample. The magazine had the time to try it out and see it work. As an added bonus, they also gave him a reader-response card number just for the asking.

In addition, he discovered that the magazine had a toll-free number so he called them to discuss his product. Generally, you won't have to go through all these steps to insure a good release. Still, it's nice to have these means available to you.

It's not going to be feasible for many of you to send a sample of your product. Instead you can send any performance tests or even testimonials from credible sources. For a service entity like Woman's Work, they have only one client but they have boosted that client's profits by thirty-five percent.

The women asked their client to write a brief letter attesting to this increase and included copies with each release-request.

Don't worry if you have no samples or testimonials to send. For the most part, unless your claims seem ridiculous, your release will run in a positive light.

Whatever you do, you should include with your release a cover letter on your letterhead. I would recommend the following format:

Date (Important)
(Addressee)

Dear (name of press release person, if available):

My company is pursuing viable avenues of results-oriented advertising and your magazine was recommended to us.

I would appreciate your running this press release and photo in your upcoming issue. If you have any questions regarding the information I have sent you, please call me at your earliest convenience.

Thank you very much for your prompt and courteous attention.

Respectfully yours,

(Your name)
(Your title)

You should now be well on your way to assembling your complete packages for your target publications. Your new packages should pack a lot more punch than your initial queries. Some of the magazines will still chop and modify but that's perfectly okay.

If, however, they inform you that they charge a small service fee to place your release, cross them off your list for now. You are offering these magazines an opportunity to grow with your venture. If they're not perceptive enough to understand that, then their business acumen is highly limited.

In keeping with our theme of "Move Forward or Rot," let's begin our advertising campaign. You've lined up your thirty magazines. Don't short change yourself on the number. We're just barely getting by with thirty. During the Olympics, I had product releases in over eight hundred magazines.

Go over your list of publications and choose six that you feel will have the greatest impact. With the balance of magazines, choose three of your consumer, trade, and general newspaper publications, nine in total. Of these nine, one should be from your high impact list. Label this as list No. 1.

Repeat this procedure with another nine magazines, except this time, choose two others from your impact list. This is list No. 2.

You should have twelve publications remaining, which include the remaining three from the high impact column. This is list No. 3.

Buy thirty 5″ x 7″ (approx.) top-folding envelopes. The larger size is used for more than just the purpose of accommodating your photo.

Within each envelope, be sure to include:
• Your cover letter and news release on your business letterhead. Each cover letter may be a photocopy or offset printed but you should affix your original signature on

each one.

- Your Product Photo, with your business card taped to the back.
- Any additional supporting documentation, with your business card stapled to each document.
- A piece of cardboard to protect the photograph.

If you're able to mail an actual sample, be sure to include the above package in your sample mailing. Don't send your sample unless it appears completely professional and refined. Get help from your local starving artist or printer, or both. If your product looks and photographs sloppily, that's tantamount to the guest of honor attending a formal gathering in a torn shirt and old blue jeans.

If your product presents itself well, but you haven't developed a container yet, at least seal it in a sealed plastic bag. When I first began shipping out product samples, I didn't have a plastic bag sealer so I used to go to my local meat market. For a few bucks, they would professionally heat seal all of my wares and never did anything smell of sirloin.

Don't let anything arrive damaged. Protect it well, if only with newspaper. Mail a couple of test shipments to yourself to see how your packaging holds up.

Address each package or envelope and always use a specific name, if available. To the lower left of the address, write the word, "P E R S O N A L" as I have spaced in and underline each letter.

If a specific name is unavailable, head the address with:
Attention: News Release Dept.
(Address)
Off to the lower left of this address, write:
DATED MATERIAL ENCLOSED.
PLEASE OPEN IMMEDIATELY.

Gather up your mailings from list No. 1 only and march on down to the post office and send them off regular postage. The post office should be adequate for most of you unless your parcel weighs enough so that a parcel service could ship it cheaper.

If you can afford the extra dollar or so, send each mailing certified mail. Though not mandatory, this type of mail can often command more immediate attention and response. Overnight mail is also highly effective if your budget allows.

Those first nine mailings should have been fairly painless on your budget. If you've followed my instructions your initial releases should begin appearing within the next two months.

After five weeks from your first mailings, send off your mailings from list No. 2. Five weeks after that, mail off to all your addressees on list No. 3.

Back to your first mailings which are now hurrying off to their respective destinations. When I carry out publicity programs like these, nearly everything I send gets published. That's what happens with a few years of experience.

When I started out, less than half of my items were published. If I had known all of the things I've shown you in this chapter, my response rate would have been much higher.

After your first mailings, do nothing for about one week. On the following week, call those magazines who have a public access toll-free number. To find most toll-free numbers, dial 1-800-555-1212.

When you call these magazines, ask them if they have received your news release and then find out when it may be published. If they need something else from you, do what you can to accommodate them, outside of paying any fees for your releases. Through these phone calls, they may find you and/or your product interesting enough to write a small article.

Generally each magazine will have a schedule revealing when they will be publishing various topics. Find out if there is a specific issue that may be ideal for the release of your product.

Many publications produce industry-related directories. These directories list all sources relevant to that industry. Often, you can get your product or service listed in these directories for free, and under many different sub-headings.

And don't forget catalogs. B. Klein Publications of Coral Springs, Florida sells an excellent directory listing 9,000 mail-order catalogs.

Often these directories and catalogs are free for the asking, especially if a publisher is trying to promote it to the industry or the general public. If that's not possible, sometimes they will send you a previously published issue for free. It is important to note however that some publishers frown upon sending out old issues because some of the information may be obsolete. What have you got to lose by asking?

All of these gratuities are really not mere give-aways. They represent an investment on the part of the various publishers in your venture as well as the future of their industry. Such investments are the kind of premiums that can really pay off for a publisher as your endeavor grows.

There is always the other side to contend with. Some of you will be told flatly that no releases are accepted or that your release will be subject to a several month waiting period.

The waiting period is no problem. Just try to get an idea of your publication date and then change over the name of this publication onto list No. 3. Then pull another publication off of list No. 3 and send it off immediately.

If they seem negative on any free news releases, be very courteous and thank them for their time. Why be kind to people who will scarcely give you the time of day? The reason should be obvious. You need to make good friends in your field and you never know when your paths may cross under very different and far more affluent circumstances.

In my years of being involved in the product-end of

marketing, there are two salesmen in particular for whom I have a tremendous admiration. They are Grady Reed, who you shall learn more about later and Lee Bardin, a general product mavin: who started with nothing but a willingness to learn and a drive to survive and now oversees an international array of breakthrough products.

They are two extraordinarily different personality types but they have one important sales technique in common. They are both keenly aware that presenting themselves as decent human beings is as important as the product they're selling. They aim to make friends and that keeps doors open.

So if the outcome isn't positive at first, if all parties involved deal with the problem responsibility and with good character, the result can pave the way to very strong future friendships.

Keep that friendship factor in mind but remember that we always try to find alternate routes leading towards our intended goal. If a publisher initially gives you the cold shoulder, wait one day and then call back. This time, ask to speak to the advertising salesperson.

Tell this person why you sent your information to the magazine and what it could mean if your press release is successful. Often times, a perceptive ad salesperson will invest a few column inches to pave the way for positive dealings in the future.

If all else fails, find out what type of editorial material they will accept and submit a small article. In the meantime, some of you may have received notes or phone calls from the various magazines. These first nine releases will give you some excellent experience on how to get you best releases out there.

It is advisable to have a few extra release packages handy in case a magazine misplaces it or if you find additional publications that you want to be in.

As you get ready for your next mailing, there may have

been some changes in your product. Modify your news release accordingly and send them away!

Your third mailing at the end of your last five-week interval should be your best. Some of your first releases should have appeared by now and you can use those releases to further perfect your presentation.

Most of you will enjoy a good degree of success with this major kick-off of your advertising campaign. Your net result is actually a cornucopia of benefits generally reserved for publicity campaigns costing several thousands of dollars.

With the help of the next chapter, you will learn how to deal with questions that can really make your jaw drop. What if a company wants to buy ten gross of your product? Who do you send samples to? What about quantity discounts and payments? What about brochures? And most importantly, how do you close the sale?

The above questions are known as "Demand Problems" and they are the best problems in the world to have. For thousands less than what is conventionally spent in advertising today, you could be on your way to a real fortune. What ever happens now, at the very least, you know that you can feasibly take any good idea and give yourself a chance to profit handsomely without having to gamble away large sums of money.

The price of making a good dream happen is good thinking, not big money!

Chapter 10

MOVING PRODUCT
The Joy of Demand

When I mentioned earlier that productivity of goods and services makes money and not the reverse, I really couldn't prove that until we reached this chapter.

Your first advertising campaign is in motion and people are beginning to ask you some confusing questions. You don't want to appear ignorant because you'll be embarrassed and you'll create doubts about the integrity of your product.

To let your own doubts cause you to give up transcends foolishness. You have something that people want. That's the bottom line. Everything else between trading their money in exchange for your goods or services, is secondary. You'll solve all the little headaches as necessary.

Generally you will not hear from the major dry goods stores, those major retail distributors. They have a purchase and distribution system that's complex enough to write another book about. I have seen these big guys buy the small guy's products but generally they have to be approached.

Your intial advertising campaign is capable of cutting through these complexities because perceptive buyers will keep their eye on certian new product sections.

You should be hearing from a number of smaller distributors and retail dealers. They will ask you about shipping, availability, pricing, quantities, etc. and you should be ready with the answers. Make a list of all your distributor, wholesale and retail pricing information, shipping dates, everything you can think of.

There are specific terms and systems that distributors use for their specific industries. Try to learn as much about your area as you can before you make or receive your first phone call. If you are confronted with something you're not sure about, tell the truth but tell it in such a way that you won't turn off the customer. Inform your customers that you will get back to them within the week with the information.

Many will ask for price lists or brochures. Though these are generally necessary tools of the trade, aim to keep your paper exchanges down to a minimum. I have written, designed and printed hundreds of brochures and as your enterprise develops, you can do a lot of fancy things. For now, just think in terms of the "PDS" or Product Data Sheet.

This will consist of a single sheet with a black and white photograph or a very good illustration, under which you shall clearly list all of your product features and benefits. This list should include product advantages over the competition, features and benefits, without revealing any secrets. Dimensions, shipping weight, quantities, should also be included.

Print only one hundred product data sheets to start out with. Build up some profit and make corrections via these first hundred before you print more. You'll also need to photocopy or quickprint price lists, one for distributors, one for dealers and one for retail customers.

When you receive calls, you can get away with simply saying, "hello" but consider some alternatives. To enhance your image, you can engage an answering service who could answer with your company name, or you could use an answering machine.

The easiest and least expensive route for now is to have all family members simply answer your home phone by stating your company name, just like an office line, unless your local phone system doesn't allow this.

The first time you saw your idea as something that you could touch or see function, it seemed like no excitement could ever top that. Compare that to the present as you actually respond to the demand you created. What began as a mere notion is now well on its way to improving your life and the lives of many others.

Hard work is a nice principle. I worked hard to develop my promotional systems. No doubt that hard work has helped many people realize certain degrees of success. But nothing beats good thinking.

Thus far, we've just scratched the surface of how to make your idea work. You have seen the beginnings of various avenues waiting for you to make use of. There's so many more exposure techniques available to you. All you need is more of that good thinking and a willingness to not limit yourself.

Chapter 11

FULL SPECTRUM MARKET PLANNING
Equal Time For The Heroes

"Full Spectrum Marketing," "Saturation" and "Market Penetration" are just a few of the terms used for the art and science of successfully getting a message out. You must do more than reach a target (intended) audience. You have to motivate them to act positively on your message.

In general, the advertising profession will cut one another's throat to win you over. Take a moment to think how much advertising has affected your own life. You can't be too fat, thin, ugly or handicapped unless an advertising campaign develops ethics of convenience for profit's sake.

It doesn't have to be that way and you can still create successful, very low-cost campaigns that work just as well. Advertising should and can be much more of a credible force in our society. You begin with a quality product or service. Then you tell the truth well.

Of course, you have to deliver that honest message through many different sources (spectrums). That is why you will incorporate the various spectrums I outline and therefore, you will increase your chances of motivating your prospects. In short, never assume that one ad or one letter, or any single spectrum will achieve your desired results.

Advertising is much bigger than most of us realize. Virtually every facet of our lives is affected by it. We are just beginning to realize the great evil and great good various advertising and public relations campaigns can create.

And the news events and people in our day-to-day lives don't just tell us what's going on, they can change the way we look at ourselves.

I have a great love for the courageous seven astronauts of

the Challenger tragedy because they represented to me America's longing to grow, reach out and be her best.

On a more earthly plane, I have a great love and admiration for people like Judy Entin, a renowned teacher of autistic children. Her work is visibly and tangibly creating a better life for these children and hence, the global village is a better place.

There are no shortages of heroes in this world. The problem is that most of us don't know where to look for them. And our quest is somewhat blinded by the business of terrorism which not only holds individuals hostage but international television as well. When a handful of terrorists strike, these murderers hijack a global audience for their cause.

Broadcasters will argue that they have an expressed responsibility to deliver the news. But what happens when they inadvertently promote and enhance terrorism and related acts of horror by making TV celebrities out of the perpetrators?

For the first half of 1986 I noticed an interesting trend in national newscasting; Tears. I noticed more teary-eyed newscasters after a sad or horrible story. Well, I guess that's a start but the next and more important step involves you. That's right, you. You're going to show the world where the media coverage really belongs; Not with acts of horror but with the little personal civic efforts that you can do to attack these problems. After all, who likes to see grown newscasters cry? Shouldn't the press play a more active role in reporting a solution?

Gary Collins' "Hour Magazine" TV show doesn't just portray victims of social ills but presents professionals who have helped to address and solve these problems. He and his producers set an excellent example of responsible and helpful reporting. He's a hero.

You are going to be part of America's real force of heroes and as a legitimate reward, your venture will profit. You've already proven that the individual who seeks out intelligent solutions can always find a way upward.

Woman's Work, Inc. wanted to incorporate their civic concerns into a viable business function. They also would love to spend twenty-thousand dollars on a modest print, radio and television campaign. The problem is they only have $341.00 in their company bank account.

They watch the news and read all the local papers. After a few weeks of "town-watching," they have come upon a community problem that they want to do something about; Child stealing and abuse.

They easily locate a couple of missing children foundations to learn various preventative techniques they can present to their young community. With the little money they have they print up special "Child I.D." cards. The cards have an area for fingerprints and photo on the front and are kept by the parents for emergency use. The women also compose a list of safety tips that they will hand out with each card. They set up an instant camera in their office and their campaign is ready to go. Now, how about a little publicity.

All that horrible, rotten news out there. Woman's Work, Inc. had one solution and they wanted equal time. They called three local television stations, one cable station and four radio stations. They related the problem and what they were doing about it.

As a result the radio stations each ran several Free public service announcements. One television station turned them down but the other two came to their office and filmed the story. Since this was a bonafide news event, both stories played on the evening news for free.

The results; scores of children with their mothers, many of whom were interested clientele. A couple of times while this three-week program was running, the police came by and volunteered time to help give fingerprints.

The women demanded equal time with the bad guys on the media and became local heroes. They made a viable and significant contribution to the community. The legimate fringe benefit of course, is community trust, credibility and a well-deserved increase in business.

One positive news story can equal scores of paid ads from the believability standpoint. Woman's Work, Inc. saved thousands of dollars in advertising costs and business became so good that they will have to hire more help.

Everyone has benefited. The community is a safer place. The company realized a success it might never have had the chance to and heightened productivity has created more new jobs. The TV and radio stations have a civic duty anyway but now their image is enhanced because they've shown their concern for the needs of the community. That's going to help their business interests.

When good solutions get equal time with the bad news, what was once a problem now becomes an opportunity. This is not just mere public relations good will stuff as the term is generally viewed. Our heroes have made a viable and active contribution to their community and through the way they proceeded, profitable results were immediate and tangible for all concerned.

The child i.d. program was the ideal choice for their business and there are thousands of other community needs. The trick is to find and address a timely topic in a manner that compels all participants to depend on your office and have a potential interest in your business.

The issues of good will or community involvement surround us. It isn't enough that donations are tax-deductible. Someone has to channel those funds and create the proper programs for recipients. If you knew just how beneficial the right involvements were, you'd take another, far more positive view of community service.

Concerning politics, I vote for the people who I feel will do the best job, be them Democrat, Republican or whatever. Currently, I look at the late Robert Kennedy's young son, Joe, with great favor.

Those who know of this young Massachusetts Kennedy are familiar with his efforts as head of the Citizen's Energy Corp., an organization that helps the poor keep their homes warm during the cold Massachusetts winter months. His efforts have actually saved scores of lives of people whose only fault was poverty. You have to love this man for the genuine good he is doing.

Since his organization is nonprofit and deeply essential to the community, he deserves and gets a lot of free TV, print and radio press. He has laid a foundation of good will and action and if he plays his cards right, he'll become a very bright star in the Kennedy legacy.

Here's another and very different example: Rock and Roll music had never really been able to shake the devil image that began in the paranoid fifties. Then, along came Bob Geldof and his production of "Feed The World." Suddenly, the music assumed focus and a conscience that raised millions of dollars and saved hundreds of thousands of lives in Africa.

His incredible life saving activities have spawned similar mass-aid activities. Giving on a global scale has become fashionable. It is incumbent upon each of us to make sure this isn't just a fad.

No one's asking you to take on the world, just the part that's somehow relevant to your venture. Give the principles in this chapter a chance to work for you. Take a good hard look at your project and put this chapter to work. You'll not only enjoy a credibility that will help build your product, you could earn enormous exposure for thousands less than it might normally cost you. And you'll deserve it.

I've had a highly successful experience marketing a group of high-quality walk-in medical centers. They had all the most advanced physician and minor surgical services. All they needed was to get the word out.

And what were those words? I determined them to be Convenience and Compassion. As a result I gave them the following slogan; "At Our Medical Centers, we don't just get you well, we treat you well."

In the beginning phases, these centers had a very limited advertising budget but needed far more exposure than they could afford.

Accordingly, my theory was to get us involved in all vital community services, from child safety, to special health-education programs. The press always responded because we were always making positive news. Best of all, the people responded, attracted initially by our compassionate image, and permanently won over once they visited us.

At one time in a town where one of these centers was situated, the local paper was doing a special magazine on drug and alcohol abuse prevention. They were selling minor sponsorships to pay for it. When they approached me, I arranged for a local radio station to do a one-hour show dedicated to the topic.

As a result, our name appeared on the cover of the magazine and we also received free radio, and even local television coverage. We became major local heroes and everyone benefited. Business again took an upward turn. Caring can be a profitable business for all concerned if structured properly. By the way, to achieve this amount of TV, radio and newspaper through standard paid advertising avenues would have cost several thousand dollars just to achieve the same exposure. Our cost for this particular campaign was only three-hundred dollars.

Even if they had ten-thousand to blow on a conventional campaign, they would never have been able to buy the credibility I gave them for three-hundred. When you just buy ads, people know you can say almost any wonderful thing you want about yourself. If, however, you carry out good deeds and work with the media properly, the people will say those wonderful things about you.

When the people draw positive conclusions about you through your good deeds, they will in turn, trust you and support your business.

We could all stand to hear a little more good news. Think how grateful your community, state or even country will be to you for making some good news. Currently and sadly, we are primarily served by the news media only in that we are relieved that the horrors aren't happening to us, as we set ourselves in front of the TV, entertained and secure but never dreaming that each one of us can make a difference.

Look again. Just in 1986, we saw a continued trend of deposed dictators, who used to be able to run their countries at will, until television exposed them to angry masses.

Marcos really met his downfall the moment he lost control of his TV station to his courageous successor.

Sometimes all news seems bad and leaves us feeling helpless but one small step to attack those problems can make all the difference in the world, especially when millions of dream-makers out there each try to do their share. Among the great fringe benefits of your own small but significant contribution is growth for your venture.

In the screwy professional world of endorsements, major athletes or other celebrities push products and causes because their elevated social status creates some degree of credibility. The irony of it all is that you can do the same thing (especially now) without having to be a superhero. Just do a good deed in your community, get the media to work with you, and you'll enjoy all the hero-credibility you'll ever need.

Don't ever be afraid to approach the media with your ideas. They are in business to serve the full spectrum information and entertainment needs of the community. Enormous, result-oriented, positive exposure can be achieved by sensible use of the media. Now you know how to build that relationship.

Camera-shy? That's fine. Stay that way. Shyness or excessive modesty can become a great crediblity tactic. Sometimes, you can remain behind the scenes all the time and let the newscasters do the work. If you do happen to get in front of a camera, be yourself and quell your fears by remembering that you have something to teach people. After a few minor experiences, you'll get used to it. As I've said all along, give yourself a chance to discover and grow with your assets.

The emphasis is on the civic event so find a cause that you can push and use it to your advantage. Your efforts will serve as another dimension of your overall campaign.

Who says you have to be rotten and heartless to be successful. Rotten and heartless people who happen to do well financially are not successful human beings and usually wind up spreading unhappiness wherever they go. When we refer to full-spectrum marketing (intelligent saturation) we must always monitor the real needs of our community.

Many years ago, when the media and money were still a mystery to me, I wrote my first book called *Skiing Without Seeing*. If you happen to see a copy around, don't buy it. It's not my most dynamic literary work.

Since my early teens, my hobby has been teaching snow-skiing to disabled skiers, specifically the blind. I was rarely paid for the thousands of hours I dedicated to this effort but it was the most rewarding experience of my young life.

I was very dedicated to it and even helped develop special techniques to give the blind more independence on the hill. The demand for ski instructors of my type grew far beyond the supply. So I wrote a book. It was released on a very small scale, as a cassette tape, accompanied by braille diagrams that attempted to outline various skiing positions.

It was written with all the style of a barely literate young punk. In fact the best writing was from Chris Peppel, a pioneer blind skier who recorded his own introduction.

I never sought out any money to put this whole venture together. Local printers and charity groups did all the assembly. Additionally, I personally distributed the package to every blind library I could locate.

Over the months of its release, there were several articles about it and I fared much better in the newspaper than on radio because I didn't understand all the attention.

Months later, I received a letter from the White House. It was a personal letter from then President Richard Nixon, Pre-Watergate. Apparently, a friend of mine had sent him a copy of *Skiing Without Seeing* in my name.

Nixon's letter praised my efforts in full "nice-job-son" style. Had I know more about marketing back then, *Skiing Without Seeing* could have made me very rich, but even though I lost money on it the value of what I did will last forever.

Eventually, I made my money on other ventures so what's the big deal about a little delay.

Consider this additional spectrum of profiting while building a better community. It comes from my friend Grady Reed and one of his companies called "The California Cookbook Company."

It's one thing to publish, promote and distribute a great cookbook but Reed took this several steps further. Witness his civic-minded approach.

He compiles the books himself. He develops a theme and then puts the word out for recipes. They come pouring in from housewives, school teachers, everyone. In addition, each book is complimented with a gorgeous array of spectacular culinary photographs. Most of these photos are contributed by major food companies, in exchange for a mention in the "acknowledgement" section. The contribution of recipes and photos saves thousands of production dollars. Why are people and corporations so generous to Mr. Reed? It's all in the selling.

He started with nothing but sincerity and conviction. Within a short time, the banks were sufficiently impressed with the man and his intentions and began funding his ventures. They have never been sorry, even though there were some iffy moments in the beginning.

He has built up a major sales force combing all the various territories throughout California and beyond. They do not, as a rule sell to conventional distribution and retail outlets although such a venture could prove highly profitable.

Mr. Reed's background is one of civic dedication and sales. His company reflects his personal philosophy. Primary sales targets are high schools where students sell his books to fund various ventures ranging from building better libraries to funding special educational trips.

His salesmen don't just dump a quantity of books at schools and then disappear. They run the entire fundraising program at each school. They teach the students how to sell the books and how to succeed.

Fundraising is another billion-dollar industry in its own right and it provides Reed a vehicle whereby he can run a strong, profitable business while improving quality wherever he ventures. He sells his books his way, the students get a terrific education about the value of selling plus they achieve a greater bond to their school.

Reed stands as an example of a great American who lives and profits from his beliefs. Thank you Grady Reed.

Still looking for an angle? Consider that your venture may be news just by the fact that it is what it is. Do you make ice cream the old-fashioned way? That's news. Are you bringing jobs to your community?

There's useful and good news in almost every venture. Once you've found it, the local print, radio or television media should not only give you free press-coverage, they should be grateful to you for your contribution.

Considering you'll be repaid ten-fold, what can you give?

Chapter 12

CO-OP ADVERTISING/SALES
Piggybacks, Coupons and Con-Jobs

You grab your mail and there it is, a windowed envelope with a check for five-thousand dollars in your name. Completely surprised, you drop everything to open the envelope. This money's really going to come in handy.

Hopes immediately fade as you behold the entire document which says, "Imagine if you saw the following in the mail:" This is followed by the now obvious dummy check but it's too late. You fell for it. You opened the envelope before throwing it away.

What about the envelopes that congratulate you for winning a free TV or the ones that warn you that your big prize is about to be cancelled. Direct-Mail organizations will tell you that this is the state of the art of this medium. If just a few percentage of the recipients respond, the effort pays off.

This is all very good and very bad. What's good is that we all love getting gifts of some sort. What's very bad is that the deceit makes us very bitter and mistrusting. We feel invaded and an increasing percentage of us are growing so numb, we are probably throwing away some real checks as well.

My father-in-law is a prominent Obstetrician/Gynecologist who has composed a newsletter addressing specialized cases in his profession. Traditionally, OBGYN's submit complicated case questions which the publisher sends to various specialists to answer.

In the past few years, the responses began falling off sharply. When followed up on, most of the potential respondents claimed they never received the questions.

Actually, they had, but the return address had only the publisher's name on it. Most thought it was junk-mail so the stuff never made it in the house. Then they began using my father-in-law's name on the envelope and guess what? The doctors are responding again.

As exemplified in the previous paragraphs, there are always innocent victims for every form of outright media deceit. So how do you get people to respond without lying? The positive avenues available could fill volumes.

The underlying premise must be honesty. You can give away gifts, specials and discounts. You can advertise this to a limited extent on the envelope of a direct-mail package. But never orient your copy so it seems to promise something that you can't really deliver. First of all, it's often illegal and secondly, your quick fix can chew away at your credibility.

The current credibility level of certain forms of direct mail may be best understood by a somewhat amusing occurrence in Ft. Lauderdale, Florida not too long ago. The premise for the following true story is that, even when people know the truth about deceitful forms of direct-mail, they may still respond positively at a 1-3% rate. Some reputable direct-mail organizations enjoy a very high response rate but many legitimate mailings receive only a 3% or lower response.

Note: Though the general story is true, I have created a fictional character based upon my own research.

The cheap wine that Joe guzzled for breakfast helped to blur out these tough nowhere days in his nowhere life. The drops of blood from last night's fight look black against the dusty green carpeting.

For the moment, he doesn't care that he punched Monica in the mouth with all the rage in the world last night, and that she's gone for good this time.

He gets up to turn on the TV and almost passes out from the acute rush of dizziness. "Click." Nothing happens, the TV does not go on. "Click, click, click, click." On-off-on-off. "What's going on here," he mumbles to himself. Then he sees the unpaid electric and other bills taped to the front of the TV. Monica did that and that's what started the fight in the first place.

How low can things get? Florida was going to be the start of his new life. The sun, the women, it was all going to happen now. The great escape from New York. A few little heists and then who knows?

Joe reached into his pocket and pulls up three crinkled dollars. He can't believe that's all the money remaining from the three-hundred and sixty dollars he grabbed at the corner gas station just a week ago.

Life couldn't take him any lower if it tried. He was sick and desperate but that part of him that wasn't scared, was far too weak to do anything.

He shuffled to the kitchen to check the refrigerator once more just to make sure it was empty. As he slides across the floor, he kicks an envelope that says on the front, "Congratulations." After staring at it for several long seconds, he grabs it and violently tears it open: "You have won a free trip to the Bahamas."

Suddenly he's alive again. Now he can really start a new life, in the Bahamas. The beaches, the women. He reads on as the letter explains that he must appear in person at a certain hotel to claim his prize on December 18, 1985, no later than 12:00 noon. "That's today, he says.

He rushes out of the apartment and flags a cab. As he arrives at the hotel, he gives the cabbie his last three dollars and tells him to wait.

Forty-five minutes later, the cabbie sees Joe and about thirty others being lead out of the hotel in handcuffs. Joe yells over to the cabbie, "I don't think you better wait for me."

Joe was one of about 3% of the respondents who fell for this giant police sting operation designed to capture fugitives. The mailing that Joe received was sent to about 2,500 fugitives but 1,000 to 1,500 of the letters were returned and marked "incorrect address, no new address known."

In addition a similar police sting operation had just been carried out a week before in another part of the country. Even with a group of thugs, who knew they were being conned, the mailing still fooled three-percent of them.

If you ever carry out a direct-mail campaign and receive a similarly low response rate, don't let anyone convince you that you should be satisfied with a low response rate.

Perhaps you have a good retail-use product or service and you're convinced that an honest mass-mailing compaign is the way to go. Should you invest several thousands to undertake a direct-mail campaign? You could wind up spending a lot of money just to turn sour on advertising. Proceed with caution and don't expect any miracles from a mass-mailing, unless your audience has either previously purchased from you or is given great incentives.

If you really think a mass-mailing will best serve your cause, try utilizing the following two money-saving tips: Instead of laying out the cost of all that postage, if applicable, see if you can pay your local newspaper to distribute your brochure as an insert. Secondly, include in your brochure a discount coupon just to introduce yourself. Direct-mailing always has a better chance when you give people a real incentive to respond.

There is a fantastic multi-billion dollar industry known as the "Ad Specialty Industry" or "Rememberance Advertising." The beauty of this industry is that it does create, manufacture and sell gifts of virtually any product with the name, address or slogan of a business firm imprinted on the product. Since specialty items are generally sold in large quantities, they are usually low-dollar products but there can be exceptions. Maybe you could approach corporations to utilize your product as an ad specialty.

Piggybacking or specials or premium offers essentially permit you to hitch a ride on a widely distributed product. You see these offers everywhere, everyday. "Special Offer," "Free Offer." On cereal boxes or any product.

Relevancy is the key. Seek out widely distributed products that might already be attracting your potential customers. Your product or service must somehow compliment but not compete with your piggyback targets.

Suppose you produce a video tour-guide of Cape Cod. Ocean Spray juices are largely a Cape Cod product. You could approach them to make a special offer of your video on some of their products. Maybe to buy your video at a special discount, the customer must include two proof-of-purchase seals from two different bottles of juice.

In theory, Ocean Spray should love it because it increases sales for their product. You really love it because your product is advertised in millions of homes for a longer period than your direct mail might have been, all at tremendous savings.

You could develop reciprocal coupon or discount agreements where the two products each offer a discount on the other. The options are as extensive as there are products and services then multiplied by each other in all combinations. What an opportunity to get it out there.

Maybe a travel magazine would co-op with you and offer your video to every new subscriber. There's no limit to whom you could approach, Win-Win. Everyone benefits and once again, you've carried out exposure for your goods or services for little or no money or risk.

What about fulfillment and supply? What if you get thousands of orders for your product? I maintained earlier that demand problems are the best problems to have. Don't prepare by overstocking but instead have resources ready should you need to switch into high gear. You'll find the fulfillment solutions. Just be sure to always work within the time frames and commerce laws governing shipping and response times.

What about those "Isn't That Amazing" direct response TV ads. Sometimes, these work quite well, especially if a small TV station is willing to take a percentage of your profits in lieu of an ad fee. Maybe they'll do the same for your conventional ads. You never know until you ask. Then go ask your attorney if it's okay.

Some popular TV game shows are seeking out particular consumer products as prizes. For little or no fee, your product could get national exposure. What have you got to lose by simply asking?

You don't need a degree or license to employ these techniques as your own just like you don't need to waste money on marketing techniques that do nothing but leave you with less money. I want you to have the success without having to spend to excess.

If you've followed my advice up to this point, you have given your idea a chance without wasting a lot of money. You can see that my greatest emphasis has been on three basic aims:

1) Free News and New Product Releases Through Print Sources.

2) Free Print, Radio and Television Publicity Through Community Involvement.

3) Free Distribution and Exposure Through Piggy-backing.

There are many marketing books on the market, all packed with an encyclopedia of advertising techniques. That has not been my intention with this book. I feel that you will best benefit by utilizing the specific techniques I have outlined.

As you grow, you may find legitimate uses for various forms of conventional advertising. But beware.

Chapter 13

CONVENTIONAL ADVERTISING
Doing It Your Way

The year was 1849. It could have been any hot summer afternoon on that dusty downtown Denver Main Street if it weren't for that sound, the one that made children, mothers, cowboys, soldiers come a runnin'.

The familiar clip-clop and clanging meant only one thing. Jeremy Jonas was a comin'.

His age was beginning to show as he tried to hide his strain as he set up his stage. He used to love the kids but he doesn't even bring em candy anymore. "Dang kids are everywhere," he shouts. "Ladies, kindly git a hold of yer dang yunggins."

As always on his monthly visit, Jeremy began with the private sales to the bar maidens as mothers covered children's eyes. The pretties paid in cash or by "services" although these days, old Jeremy preferred cash. He was getting too old and now he just wanted to take the four-hundred dollars he had saved up over the years and get a ranch and stop scurrying.

The biggest sales always came at the end, the one's that made him famous throughout the southwest. The crowd swelled as Jeremy began an act he could perform in his sleep.

"Dear ladies, have you been feeling a bit extra worried lately? Is the mister not givin' you the attention he used teh? Gentlemen, are you feeling tired when you wake and even worse when you get home?"

Groans of acknowledgement spark the dank surroundings as he continued. "My dear friends, you don't have to feel that way, not if you use my miracle elixir. My special elixir isn't like any other." His enthusiasm builds as the crowd gets more excited. He's got em. Time to close in for the kill.

"For a mere twenty-five cents, that's right, just twenty-five cents, my special tonic can work miracles for you and your family."

A voice cried out, "I'll take a bottle," followed by a sea of hands and the kind of commotion that makes Jeremy's innards smile. The noise of the crowd blocked out the rush of the hoof-beats. By the time Jeremy recognized them, it was too late.

As they grabbed him, they fired a few shots in the air to quiet the crowd. The scruffiest of the group held up a bottle of miracle elixir as he spoke, "This here miracle elixir done killed my little girl. It ain't nothing but whisky, turpentine and oil from some ol' sidewinder (rattlesnake)."

Shaking, Jeremy whispers to the man. "I got four-hundred dollars in the wagon. Let me go and it's all yours."

It seemed like just a few seconds between when the noose went around poor Jeremy's neck and when the cowboy slapped the horse out from under him. This time, the mothers let their children look on.

Nowadays we don't hang snake-oil salesmen. We rush them $19.95. Daily some advertiser finds another group of suckers. Sometimes they get caught, but most of the time, they take the money and run.

We ad execs, marketers, salesmen, etc. can be a very pushy lot. After all sales is the lifeblood for all of us and we have to survive with whatever techniques are available to us. Obviously, the bigger the package we sell, the more money we make.

Yet how many ad agencies are willing to talk about the big money campaigns that didn't succeed? Believe me, that side of it is not a very glorious experience. Now there are many brilliant advertising people out there. Still the only guarantees they can make are to give you their best efforts within the constraints of their own technology.

Time to bust out of those constraints. Things must change. The media must be more responsible and responsive at all levels. Even successful tycoons must rethink the massive advertising expenditures that they formerly favored simply because it seemed to work. Even for a successful campaign that costs One-Hundred Million dollars, what if the same powerful results could be realized for a fraction of that fee? Then companies would have more profit to expend on research, development and other high-growth areas.

And the little guy who never had the means to succeed now has those means. That's what progress is all about, a better, more efficient way that creates more opportunities and growth for everyone.

We're still after great success in fact, we're after even greater successes but at a more efficient and intelligent cost.

From that littlest inventor looking for a chance, to the great CEO's seeking a better use of communications and sales technology. It's reorientation time and the revolution begins with each and every one of you. From now on you control your advertising expenditures so more profit goes to you instead of people like me.

Your Full Spectrum marketing will cover all the angles, or pieces of the pie, to assure the success of your venture. Major agencies may push this marketing concept under many different names and their definitions can be very limited.

Full Spectrum marketing has a different meaning for every venture. But for each you must make legitimate use of every free or economical marketing technique available to you, in order to reach every facet of your buying public (market).

You must also seek out useful and relevant community

themes that effectively bond the various forms of media with the side benefit being the growth and development of your venture.

This chapter will give you enough of a base to understand how to separate the snake-oil salesmen from the legitimate sales and marketing people. I want you to learn how to shop carefully and effectively.

Some marketing people will use this book to enhance and compliment their already-good techniques so the numbers of competent advertising people are increasing daily.

As the advertising industry tells the public all the time, "Why pay more?" You can ask them the same question. Why should you ever pay more for advertising that will not achieve any better results than you may now be enjoying.

Even for the least expensive venture, we have saved thousands of dollars in the birth stages during that critical first year. Still once you've reached some semblance of cruising speed, don't feel compelled to run to the first conventional ad agency that woos you.

No matter what has happened to your concept in its first year, the ad execs would have taken the profits that should have belonged to you. Even if you lost money and went down in debt and defeat, they would have made money.

There are extremely valid advertising services and agencies out there but you must never approach them as hopeless and helpless. My systems give thousands more ventures a chance to happen. That's better for you and your increased successes are better for our economy. There's nothing stronger than personal excitement and incentive. No one has taken your money, spent it and left you hanging. You're too smart for that now.

By employing my systems, you've given your venture a great running start but suppose your project now mandates massive paid exposure. Though not necessarily inevitable, sometimes agency services are needed.

Before you choose an agency, be certain you have gone as

far as you can go using my techniques because they do work. After several months of positive growth indicators, try recycling some of my publicity techniques. Are you continuing to build your image as a source and authority in your field?

You could attempt a different angle with the magazine program or submit articles or editorials explaining (or be interviewed about) how your concept has improved things. Have you exhausted the piggyback possibilities?

My first rule about ad agencies: Use them intelligently, only when you need them. Use wisdom in determining your advertising plans and not the expenditure of high dollars as the key ingredient.

An ad agency who insists that buying tons of ads is the best way to go, or who does not start out with a ton of research, or who insists on a long-term retainer should all immediately draw your suspicion.

If an agency specializes in only one form of advertising, like just newspaper, for example, what do you think they're going to tell you to do? Similarly, many radio, magazine, or newspaper advertising salespeople could approach you with the same pretense about the form of media they represent. That's a lot of what today's sales are all about. Be careful, don't believe everything you see and hear, you already knew that. But don't ever believe the statistics they show you unless you can verify that they are unbiased.

Agencies should serve you when you need them to fulfill a specific task and should not create a steady draw against your profits. Larger long-term campaigns could mean an exception but still, watch how your money is spent.

Advertising implies risk. Although some agencies and systems have better track records than others. Some call this risk an investment but how many agencies will guarantee a return on that investment?

Yes, you often have to take a chance to succeed but sometimes agencies will take the risk with you. Personally, I always do so with my larger clients as a statement of belief in my work.

If an agency or an ad exec really believes his ads will succeed, ask that person to give you a month's worth of free ads to test his promises. If those free ads work and you make money, you could consider a limited test run for a similar period of time.

You may also be able to trade your goods and services for advertising time, either directly or through a third party who would accept your item and in turn provide the advertiser with a needed service. In exchange for receiving that product or service directly from you or from another provider that you paid with your goods or services, you will receive advertising space or time.

There are folks who will make just such an investment in you but generally, most agencies don't have that kind of faith in their results. Now there are definite exceptions to this type of contingency program. For example, larger agencies who maintain a staff to serve large concerns can't afford to take such risks no matter how good they are. However, there's nothing stopping that agency from trying some spot contingency programs as indicators of what could happen on a larger scale.

Agencies receive fees in the form of commissions, retainers and/or salaries. Their systems of compensation vary. You also have the option of setting up an in-house agency. Or maybe you've become so proficient at your marketing, that you are all the agency you'll ever need.

You hire an ad agency for one thing only; Results. How they go about achieving those results varies and can make the difference between your success and failure. That's why you should have an authoritative hand in how they spend every penny.

Most importantly, if they have not read this book, you may find yourself talking way over their heads. Make sure they get a copy. Those few dollars they spend on it could make all the difference in the world for a successful profitable relationship with you and other successes-to-be like you.

Once they have read the book, you still must shop carefully. If you're seeking out a certain specific form of the media, still make sure you're only paying for what you need. Let's say you want to develop a TV ad to run on a local station, do you really need an entire agency for that? Maybe you just need a video production company or a top student from a communications college. Or maybe that local TV station can produce what you need for free or at a discounted rate since you're already buying time. If you do break down and buy ads in any form of media, make sure that particular medium gives you a healthy share of free additional P.R., news, article space, whatever is relevant to your situation. If your product does something for someone or something else anywhere, there's also a news event hiding in there somewhere.

When seeking out advertising services, cut out all unnecessary middlemen. Don't pay for a chain of services you don't need. A clever advertising man can advertise himself much deeper into your wallet than you really want. Shop around. As you've already seen, the exact same or better results can be realized for less if you just learn how to shop.

Once you've selected an outside agency or yourself as your in-house agency, begin with research. If the agency is smart they'll ask you all kinds of questions about you and your product, your dream. Some of the queries will seem very sophisticated, some will seem very stupid. Be patient and answer each question with respect.

As they research, they are developing a proposal, for which you should not have to pay for unless you execute it. The formation of a proposal or marketing plan can take a few days or a couple of months, depending on the size and scope of your venture.

Assembling a marketing proposal or plan is not a burden for a professional. The plan will also demonstrate how well that agency understands Full Spectrum Marketing. You'll know very quickly whether they've read my book or not. Study the plan. Spend a week with it. Never make decisions right at the presentation when emotions may cloud your ability to make rational, cost-effective determinations.

Look at their fees and project what they could cost you over a year's time. Will you be locked into them even if the relationship falters? Are they taking on some of the work that you are already proficient at yourself?

They may show you some artwork, slogans or body copy (the writing that comprises the ad). As you review all this material, you have to keep asking yourself, "How will this all work to sell my product?" If you're reading a lot of cute copy or medium-funny jokes, a warning-flag should go up.

Humor and cute can work extremely well but it requires a very special talent. Intended humor could be taken as cruel by certain groups. You can be sure that reprimands are often handed out or follies are abashedly exposed by any number of regulatory or special interest groups.

When I used to try my hand at humor with clients, I always got a kick out of myself, and generally some chuckles from my clients or prospects. Though there was the time I suggested the following slogan to a birth-control products company: "We Don't Deliver." It drew laughs from everyone on the board except for the women, most of whom were not amused.

To make it worse, I later learned that I was not the first with this cute pun. It then occurred to me why it's often felt that puns can be the lowest form of humor. First of all, they can simply be unfunny and worst of all, many others may have already discovered that same silly phrase long before you did.

On the other hand, people eat up good puns, like the famous Skip Morrow greeting cards. The key is cleverness and originality.

Once I created a line of blue jean labels. They were cute-looking things that were to be sewn over existing labels. The name of my jeans were "Who Cares." That joke worked.

One last indulgence in my own vanity regarding a hot-tub company I used to work for. As you know hot-tubs make lots of bubbles. So I made bubble gum and wrappers that read, "For Your Best Bubbles, Chews (Name of Hot-Tub Company)." We handed them out at a couple of trade-shows and they pulled in a lot of customers.

Okay, no more. I promise, except for the band-aids I once made for a Walk-In medical center, upon which I imprinted, "(Name of Business), Gauze We Care."

If you're feeling kind of ill right now, you understand my point about puns. If you're laughing hysterically, then I'm really worried about you. Be careful with cute stuff.

Headlines and slogans and art are what initially attract your reader or listener. Don't lose them.

As we get into copywriting, remember, don't offend people or even your competition. I know you see it done all the time from major competitors. That perplexes me because offensive tactics are remembered long after the product or message have been forgotten. If you knowingly insult people's intelligence, they'll ultimately seek revenge by losing faith in what you say. Even if they depend on your product, they'll now seek an alternative if one ever comes up. In sum, blatant offenses in any manner ultimately create new competition.

Good copywriting tells the truth in such an appealing, credible and informative manner, that the readers are motivated to buy. It's easy to stray away from that ideal since advertising and creative writing are so interrelated and multi-dimensional.

Try writing some ad copy yourself. You could be very pleasantly surprised. After all, you've already done some writing. Your magazine releases are an excellent place to draw ideas from. You can also draw from your experiences in making sales presentations. What did you say to win them over? You know your audience. Begin by writing to them just as you talk to them.

Grab that old trusted friend and persuade him to believe what you're selling. Get it down on paper. A good friend will not be afraid to give you harsh criticism if you deserve it and that could prove very helpful. Whoever writes the copy, here are some additional standard pointers that they may want to integrate.

When new advertising students come to me they always blurt out the word, "AIDA" or "AIBA" or "AIDCM."

These strange-looking words are actually letter groupings that roughly spell out the following advertising formulas:

AIDA = 1. Attention
       2. Interest
       3. Desire
       4. Action

AIBA = Same sequence with the B of Believability.
or
AIDCA = Same sequence with a C for Credibility.
or
AIDCM, with M for Motivation.

In turn, I'm supposed to be impressed that they can pick that up from a textbook. But can they write? Can they live with and sensitize themselves to a product and make me understand and believe what they're saying? Most importantly, can they enhance their writing from valid criticism and mistakes?

If yes to all of the above, and most importantly, if their work makes money, then I don't care what formula they can recite. You and I are only interested in ethical, cost-effective results.

Formulate a plan. Incorporate only the professionals you really need for only the time you need them. Rework and revise that plan as you progress and discover better paths.

If you're even considering a relationship with an ad agency, chances are you're making some money and want to make more. As you begin to realize significant profits, you'll run into two categories of business people. The first type will protect and enhance your earnings. The second type will take your money and do very little else. Keep your eyes open.

I have labeled much of today's advertising as ineffective and overweight. You, and thousands like you are using this guide to render the dinosaurs obsolete.

Agencies currently employing the systems I have layed out will love this book but the antiques who must now make major changes will scream loudly. That screaming is a good sign of an agency unwilling to learn and grow.

Eventually and collectively, you will render this book obsolete. And then you know what will happen? With your help and feedback, I'll write a new one.

Chapter 14

WORKCHART
The Talking Checklist

There have been a lot of changes in reference and business text books in the past several years. Publishers discovered that if they cut out the boredom, they could really broaden readership.

Suddenly we can enjoy a healthy taste of ventures that used to scare and confuse us. Americans are getting smarter and are hence able to do more on their own.

Nowadays for every book of this nature, there's usually an audio version, a video version and even a workbook. That can add up to a lot of money just to absorb some technique.

As I said in the beginning, I don't want you to go bankrupt from buying a flood of how-to literary artillery. The point is to give you useful hands-on techniques that you can get out there and use.

I can't include supplemental videos in this initial package. That would make the cost prohibitive and also those things are essentially unnecessary at this point.

I can include a consolidated workchart as a means to insure your progress. As your venture develops, refer to the workchart especially when you get stuck. The chart can help you get going again quickly and effectively.

As you work with the chart, make notes at the headings that represent your challenge points. You want to learn from mistakes, you don't want to forget and repeat them.

Get to it.

THE BRONSON WORKCHART

The workchart lists all steps to your venture's success as outlined in the book. Under the headings and subheadings, anticipated problems are listed with accompanying solutions.

1. FINDING YOUR IDEA
   A. Think about likes and dislikes.
   B. Begin to make notes about your random and fragmented thoughts.
   C. Make a three-stage wish.
      1) Get past simply wishing for money, or becoming a wealthy vegetable.
      2) Complete the following sentence: "I wish I could......"
      3) Use the book to turn that passion into reality.

Problem: Can't find an idea.

Solution: Fear of failure for those who have formerly tried and failed before is understandable but then again, you never had this book to help you before either.

Fear of failure from those who have never tried a venture before is less understandable. First of all, you know some failures are unavoidable components of eventual success. Secondly, how are you going to know what you've got unless you give it a try?

Since I've attempted to take most of the financial risk out of it, the worst that can happen is you enhance your education about something and thus increase your value as a human being.

Assert your right to become a full and fulfilled soul. Don't be shy.

Hitting upon the wrong idea generally results from bad listening or unrealistic planning. If you're building a boat, you don't begin by building a QE2.

Work and grow within your gifts and abilities. Even something new must have a characteristic that somehow reflects that which has always been a part of you.

2. TESTING YOUR IDEA

A. Pick brains of all the various levels of people related to your idea.
B. Assure proper protection for your idea, if applicable. Consult with attorney if applicable.
C. Seek honest criticism.

Problem: Insecure about releasing the idea without sufficient patent protection.

Solution: People generally have the following choices once they have received their patents: They can sell the idea, lease it, they can put the patent certificate on a shelf to show their grandchildren, or they can make the venture happen themselves.

Though many of you do require exacting protection, review all the alternatives with your attorney. Get your protection and then move ahead. In my experience, I have seen paranoia kill more ideas than even greed kills.

Your other innate protection is that, for most cases, no one has your specific technical skills to make your venture successful. This book has shown you that you have things of far greater value to offer your prospects i.e. your know-how from concept all the way to customer.

Problem: Can't find authorities to talk to.

Solution: For simple products or ideas, it's just a matter of time before you track down the right people. The only problem may be distance.

If you live too far away from the right people, don't just send your product with a letter. Before you run up huge phone bills, see if your target company has a public access toll-free phone number.

If your venture is fairly sophisticated, break it down into components and seek out the makers of those individual components.

You can also locate products with some similarities to yours which might be marketed in a fashion similar to yours. Those experts could also benefit from your marketing prowess.

Problem: Afraid or unable to approach these experts.

Solution: People are people first, just like you. Many of this country's biggest success stories were once nothing but an idea, maybe like yours. Those types often welcome someone with a similar ambition.

If someone refuses to meet with you, after much effort on your part, move on. After you've succeeded, let them come crawling to you.

If someone acts in a very intimidating manner towards you, don't be affected by it. You are there for knowledge. If you have to cut the meeting short, leave politely and seek your information elsewhere. There are plenty of successful human beings out there who can help you and who will treat you with respect.

3. DEVELOPMENT AND ASSESSMENT

A. Create a model.

1) Locate and organize resources to assemble model and/or written proposal.
2) If any fees are involved, get a full understanding of what they are in advance.
3) Be extremely clear when telling any artists, or other venders what you are looking for.
4) Continually check on progress.

B. Present your model to heavies for "High Critique Grand Rounds."

1) Get their best criticism.
2) Research-Refine-Research-Refine.
3) Keep increasing the value of your product and service.

Problem: Can't make a model.

Solution: If you feel you just can't put together some kind of model or written description, you may need to do more homework.

With sufficient knowledge, you should be able to put something together if you're really serious about your idea.

Re-examine your sources. Someone may be giving you misleading or unqualified advice which is creating an obstacle for you.

Problem: Can't get anything on paper.

Solution: Even if you're barely literate, if you can relate any thoughts to other people, you can find help to get those words clearly on paper. Break through this fear and give your venture a chance to succeed.

4. PREPARATIONS FOR TESTING THE MARKET

   A. Don't lose control of your product.
      1) If you sell or lease your idea, maintain a degree of participation in the marketing areas.
   B. Write your press releases.
      1) Be simple and clear in your product descriptions.
      2) Describe what it is and does (features) and how your improvements will benefit the user.
      3) Include no photos at this time.

Problem: Project seems too overwhelming and burdensome.

Solution: Everything is big when we look at the whole picture at one time and new things can seem a bit scary at first. So tackle the component issues piece by piece.

No one is asking you to attack it all at once. When you feel tired and frustrated, walk away from it all. Reapproach it later with a clear head and a refreshed attitude.

Sometimes people get too rigid and impose impossible goals and deadlines on themselves. That kind of activity is merely a clever way of "flunking" yourself out of and escaping from responsibility.

Your project is an important part of you. Keep the faith and perspective.

Problem: Can't write those initial news release paragraphs.

Solution: Call a local paper, newsletter or magazine and ask them to do a small news writeup on your venture. Adopt and modify that copy for your other releases.

5. DON'T GET STUCK

    A. Move forward.
        1. Find out what's paralyzing you and get around it.
    B. Don't let old patterns hold you back.
        1. Approach your venture as an adventure and not a fear.
    C. If it's holding you back, find a way to get around it.
        1. Sometimes the only way to alter negative behavior is to put all the deep analytical thinking aside and just alter the behavior!

Problem: Losing confidence in moving forward.

Solution: A fear is defined as anything we perceive as a fear. One person's boogey-man is another person's angel.

Your lack of confidence is robbing you of your chance to get ahead and become a more fulfilled human being.

You may need to modify your idea into something more interesting and motivating. Reread Chapter 1 and see if your rebirth winds you up in the same place.

If you can't inspire yourself and you're still really stuck, ask a friend for honest support. If you need more of a boost, sometimes a clergyman can help.

If not, don't be at all ashamed or embarrassed to see a psychologist once or twice. Many of this country's greatest business people and leaders often use the services of a corporate or other type of psychologist. Everyone can face challenges of growing and coping.

Any counseling that will get you unstuck and keep your idea alive, may also yield the fringe benefit of helping to make you a happier person.

Your project in itself can serve as excellent therapy because it can help to validate your essence. Give it a chance.

Find and develop your own special formula to move forward to each succeeding step. And, of course, you may always contact my organization via a Bronsultation described at the end of this book.

6. EVALUATING MARKET RESPONSE
   A. Submit your news releases for publication.
   B. Follow up with phone calls, when necessary.
   C. Seek out additional areas for media release, if applicable.
   D. Evaluate responses.
   E. Throw a party.
   F. Determine how your respondents helped you to make a better product.

Problem: Fear of using the media.

Solution: Admittedly, it can seem like a scary prospect but once you've first done it, it becomes easy and fun.

That local media is there to reflect news in your community. Your venture is news. Find the angle and spread the word to the best of your abilities.

Problem: No responses to your media blitz.

Solution: It is extremely rare for no one to talk to you about your release. First, make sure your releases have been mailed, received and published.

Your release may be unclear, especially if this is your first venture. Did you get all the help you needed to get your message out in an understandable fashion? If readers are at all confused they'll pass it by.

Submit revised and corrected releases to the exact same publications. Explain what you think happened the first time around and ask for a second chance.

If everything checks out yet you still receive no responses, call some of your friends and pick their brains. Send clippings of your write-ups to potential manufacturers, distributors, etc. and follow-up with phone calls.

Problem: Everyone's saying it's impossible for the little guy to make it against the big guys.

Solution: I have a book and a successful career that proves them wrong. Find the factors that will make your idea possible.

Impossible can often be a stupid word. There is always some way to address the issue. Ridiculous, however is a word you may want to listen to if you hear it a lot. If your venture is heading in the wrong direction, seek out the best advice you can muster and straighten it out and put those big guys in their place.

Be persistent with a good idea but don't be stubborn about making a necessary change.

Problem: Production and/or implementation seem too complicated.

Solution: Venders and suppliers want to make money. If you can work with them to develop a marketable product, their heightened interest will help keep the assembly phase alive.

Problem: Can't put it together in America.

Solution: You probably haven't shopped around enough. American suppliers go bankrupt daily because they lack sufficient financial creativity to keep making their goods in this country.

My international clients tell me that my excessive pro-Americanism deprives developing nations the chance to develop. I am sensitive to the world's needy and I do understand that the older jobs are replaced with jobs for our new technology. But such transitions can render people unemployed for years. Americans deserve better protection than that.

How can you and an American manufacturer team up to put your concept together in a cost-effective manner? Profit sharing? Other incentives?

Don't head overseas unless you've really exhausted all the possibilities, or unless yours is a task that might best benefit a developing country far more than the U.S. But be sensitive to the labor needs of your business community.

7. PRODUCTION PLANNING

A. If applicable, entertain offers from co-venturers.
1) Aim to remain involved with each phase of your product's development and sale.
2. Utilize only the services you need.
B. Develop a feasible test-market.

Problem: Can't find a manufacturer that you feel comfortable with.

Solution: Sometimes, you'll encounter some very ruthless but successful folk that you just can't bring yourself to trust no matter how much money they may promise you. Pass them by. In the long run, you'll find it more profitable to work with a better communicator.

If you must work with someone who you fear may neglect their commitments, try to anticipate the worst thing they might do regarding your idea. Have a lawyer draft up the proper protective agreement and then proceed with a polite but tight leash.

Problem: Project is not suitable for field-test.

Solution: Virtually everything can be tested. Essentially, an idea is a theory and a theory is a model of something that may or may not work. Have you done everything possible to prove or insure the success of your theory before you go into mass production?

Once people see their product or idea ready to assemble, over-anxiousness often takes over at a time when common sense and logic is needed most.

A small test can prevent a large failure. Be sure to create as many success indicators as possible. And LISTEN to your results. Why do you think the gathering of information is called the gathering of intelligence?

8. PRICING, SALES AND DISTRIBUTION.
   A. Determine pricing.
      1. Establish fair and competitive pricing.
      2. Try to avoid using price as the main selling point.
      3. Emphasize quality of goods or services.
   B. Go back and sell your product to your test-market.
      1. Offer these individuals a generous reduced rate.
   C. Determine most appropriate distribution avenues.
      1. Talk to major retailers.

Talk to distributors relevant to your market.

Problem: No confidence in selling your concept.

Solution: You have defined your goals and now must become comfortable with your project. You must believe in what you're doing or no one else will.

Be flexible and don't expect to make every sale you attempt. Learn from each prospect as to increase your chances for success with your next prospect. Some of your best experiences will emanate from your sales experiences as you discover first hand what distributors and/or general public will and will not buy from you.

Problem: Can't come up with a competitive price.

Solution: Some products or services command higher prices than others in a similar category. Price can be measured by what a willing buyer will pay to a willing seller. If you have a superior concept, price won't be the major issue.

If your product is similar to existing ones except yours costs more, why should people pay more for almost the exact same thing? Take a careful look at your competition and determine what features you could create to stand out and thereby merit a higher price tag.

Reexamine your manufacturing and distributing costs. These entities don't want to overprice themselves out of business. If necessary, get them to bend at least for the first six months of production.

Problem: Can't find a distributor.

Solution: All goods are distributed somehow. A call to a couple of disinterested distributors means nothing. There are thousands of distributors and an equal number of creative distribution options.

You have to attract, persist and sell them at a price that must guarantee a profit for yourself. Consider all cost factors carefully.

Your first ad campaign can create a number of options that could build some sales volume, after which time you could be in a stronger position to approach a distributor.

9. CREDIBLE, ALMOST-FREE ADVERTISING THAT WORKS

   A. Locate appropriate publications for your news releases.
   B. Write credible product or service descriptions.
   C. Acquire a good photograph.
   D. Submit news release packages as outlined in this chapter and according to the prescribed timetable.

Problem: Can't locate the right special interest publications.

Solution: This is very unusual. I have never known of a product or concept that didn't have a related publication of some sort. You need to carry out better homework.

Your local librarian should at least be able to point you in the right direction. Make certain you have checked out any related industries or retail businesses. Try the Yellow Pages.

Check the newsstands and ask the magazine stores if they can look up your related topics in their order books.

Problem: Can't get anything published.

Solution: Seek out additional magazine sources. Find out why your items have been rejected and make the proper corrections.

For any aspect of our society, there's a form of media that represents it. Stretch your imagination. Get your news out there.

10. MOVING PRODUCT

A. Answer all inquiries honestly.
1. Pledge to research what you do not know.
B. Have basic information sheets available.

Problem: No responses to your promotional campaign.

Solution: Some responses can take a few months, others will contact you right away. If most of your releases have been published, and you still have received no inquiries, there may be something in your photo or your writing that's turning them off. Have you been careful to clearly portray your product as an improvement over the competition?

Give each spectrum of your campaign a chance to integrate and deliver. After all three phases of your release-mailings, if things aren't at least beginning to click, reread Chapters 1 and 2. You may have missed something in concept development. Were you honest about the test results? Did you make the appropriate corrections or was your mind already made up before you began testing. Bad listening makes incomplete ideas.

Problem: Good responses but unsure how to handle them.

Solution: The delightful dilemma. Chances are you'll make some money under these circumstances. If just to close those first few crucial deals, hire an expert in your field on a temporary basis as a last resort.

Essentially, your prospects will be more concerned about your ability to follow-up than on a wealth of knowledge and experience.

Whatever you do, don't lose the sale.

Problem: Overwhelmed with too many orders.

Solution: First of all, congratulations. Now don't blow it. Run to that local manufacturer and/or distributor and show them your flood of orders.

Or...many successful ventures used a garage or living room as the first office or production plant. You could develop your own fulfillment (product delivery) system and hire local high school students to help with the process.

Those orders mean money is waiting out there with your name on it.

11. FULL SPECTRUM MARKET PLANNING.

A. The community hero campaign.
   1) Seek out examples in the media of promoted community services, charities, etc.
   2) Determine the best community cause you can best champion with your product.
   3) Develop a plan which clearly shows you and your product aiding that cause.
   4) Develop all free media avenues to publicize your interwoven cause.

Problem: Can't find a relevant civic project.

Solution: There are always issues that need desperate attention. Just ask your clergyman, social worker or police officer.

Indeed, you want people to buy your goods or services on their own merits. Somehow your product improves somebody's life. If it's something for a handicapped person, that is ideal media material in its own right.

If your idea is a better widget with no civic relevancy, that doesn't prevent you from doing something to increase your prospects' impression of you. As the respect increases, more people will believe in what you're selling. Consider a well-publicized donation of your product to a needy group.

It's important that you are genuine with your endeavor so find a cause you can be sincere about.

12. CO-OP ADVERTISING AND SALES

A. Find a related product you can approach for a piggy-back mailing.

B. Explore all exposure and distribution avenues that can display your product without draining your bank account.

Problem: Getting discouraged about making a good piggy-back-distribution contact.

Solution: Never pin your hopes on just one or two possibilities or you'll be a slave to their requisites. Try to create ten viable options for each program.

Even if a company rejects your idea at first, find out what changes you could make and resubmit.

Problem: Can't find any piggyback-distribution possibilities.

Solution: Finding the right one can take some time. This chapter tries to scratch the surface of piggyback options available to you. New systems pop up every day.

13. CONVENTIONAL ADVERTISING

A. If using any aspect of a conventional ad agency, make sure you know what you're buying.
   1) Pay for only the services you need.
B. Attempt to structure a results-oriented contingency program.
C. Be sure the writing serves the need to sell the product.
D. Begin your relationship by having the agency read this book.

Problem: The ad people insist that the programs in this book do not work.

Solution: I would say the same thing if my livelihood were threatened.

Asking an ad exec to substantiate his discontent is not an unreasonable request. If they can give your product the same momentum and credibility in the first six months as cheaply and effectively as I can, then give them three-hundred dollars for the full six months to prove it.

By the way, prepare to say goodbye to that three-hundred dollars and much more. Please don't spend more than you have to, as opposed to what they say you have to spend.

New and better ideas integrate with the old to enhance them.

You can't begin to imagine what people will promise when it comes to selling an advertising account. Let the garbage roll off your shoulders and keep your perspective. A promise is not a promise unless it is in writing and signed by the authorized and participating parties.

The advertising profession consists of persons from every imaginable profession. The only experts are those whose cost-effective techniques work for you.

If you've never met advertising people, you may be enthralled by the first one you meet. That's why you should meet several to gain the best perspective.

14. WORKCHART

Problem: Workchart seems too complicated to follow.

Solution: Use only the segments you need and always work through one concept at a time until you fully understand it. If you positively do not understand a point or have a specialized problem for your venture, see the Bronsultation page at the book's end.

TIME TO MAKE YOUR GOOD IDEAS COME TO LIFE

Each of us is born with certain gifts. The trick is to find and develop those gifts. No matter the age, social status or previous track record, it's never too late or too early to find and grow with your real talents. Percentage-wise, there are more unhappy rich than unhappy poor people. There's no greater wealth than one which stems from discovering and growing with your own natural gifts.

The first step is to discover your best ideas and then instead of reacting to life, you can act upon your dreams.

Every idea, every proposal, every lead is completely worthless without sufficient follow-up and exploration that achieves each step of your plan. Without that follow-up, you may as well never have started in the first place.

During our formative years, most of us were continually reinforced for every effort we made. We were told that trying was more important than the results. That's fine for growing up and learning but not for real idea-builders.

In the real world, only results count and all the empty promises delay the success that's waiting for you. It's far better to say, "I have done," than "I am going to do." Otherwise we are merely fishing for childlike gratification.

Each of you has a separate and unique opportunity to profit greatly from your dream. The more you can focus your energies on completing each step, the more you will profit.

If your concept requires meetings, make sure those meetings are creating profit. Proceed at your own pace and style but channel your energies toward achievement.

We live in a world where the right knowledge transforms any dream into a possibility. Take this book and make your best dreams happen. Make your best self happen. Don't just wish or hope for a better world, make a better world. Let your strengths overcome your weaknesses and let yourself grow.

My intention has been to help make all good dreams possible. That's the ideal that built this country and it's a wonderful principle.

Have I promised you instant riches like all those miracle ads that take advantage of your right to hope? Of course not! Profit motive does not forgive deceit.

Could my ideas make you rich or famous? Indeed I do have some clients who have used my techniques and become millionaires but my goal has been to see you become more fulfillment-oriented than merely money-oriented. You could make a lot of money but why just have things of value if you haven't developed values?

Get out there and make things better in your own way. Have fun. Maybe you will get rich. My wish for you, however is that this book has helped your venture give you a more enriched life.